●●●●● The Portfolio Book

The Portfolio Book

A Step-by-Step Guide for Teachers

Elizabeth F. Shores
Cathy Grace

PEARSON

Merrill
Prentice Hall

Upper Saddle River, New Jersey
Columbus, Ohio

The Portfolio Book

Dedication

To Finos B. Johnson and Charles C. Grace,
with gratitude for their support.

Vice President and Executive Publisher: Jeffery W. Johnston
Editor: Julie Peters
Editorial Assistant: Michelle Girgis
Director of Marketing: Ann Castel Davis
Marketing Manager: Autumn Purdy
Marketing Coordinator: Tyra Poole

This book was printed and bound by Phoenix Color Book Group. The cover
was printed by Phoenix Color Corp.

Pearson Education Ltd.
Pearson Education Singapore Pte. Ltd.
Pearson Education Canada, Ltd.
Pearson Education–Japan

Pearson Education Australia Pty. Limited
Pearson Education North Asia Ltd.
Pearson Educación de Mexico, S.A. de C.V.
Pearson Education Malaysia Pte. Ltd.

10 9 8 7 6 5 4 3 2 1
ISBN: 0-13-170534-2

Table of Contents

The Portfolio Book

Table of Contents

The Portfolio Book

Acknowledgments

In one sense, every child, caregiver, teacher, parent and administrator either of us has talked with or observed is a part of this book. We thank everyone who has spent time with us over the years and across the miles.

Numerous people have given us concrete help with this project. We want to thank Pam Schiller for encouraging us to write this book and Larry Rood, Leah Curry-Rood and Kathy Charner of Gryphon House for accepting it.

The following persons and organizations were also extremely helpful:

administrators and teaching staff of Tupelo, MS, Public Schools;

teaching staff and children of Lift Head Start in Tupelo, MS;

Ann K. Levy of the Educational Research Center for Child Development at Florida State University;

Betty Raper, Principal of Gibbs Magnet School for International Studies and Foreign Languages in Little Rock, AR, and her faculty, particularly Carolyn Blome, Susan Turner Purvis, Kristy Kidd, Kayren Grayson Baker, Bea Kimball, Sherry Weaver, Patricia Luzzi and Don Williams;

Jane Beachboard of Little Rock, AR, whose extensive experience with young children with special needs, thorough theoretical knowledge and sense of humor are inspirational;

Nancy Livesay of SERVE (SouthEastern Regional Vision for Education); the Arkansas Humanities Council; all of the participants in the ERIC early childhood listserve (Elizabeth 'lurked' around that on-line discussion group for months, learning something from every writer's comment);

Cynthia Frost and the interlibrary loan department of the Central Arkansas Library System;

Kelly Quinn of Little Rock, AR; and

Beverly Sandlin of Okaloosa-Walton Community College in Niceville, FL.

P.S. We would like to hear from you about how portfolios work in your community. Send letters, entries from your teaching journals, series of work samples, photographs, parent newsletters, newspaper articles and other materials to us, care of Gryphon House. If we receive enough information, we will compile it in a follow-up to this book, so be sure to include complete details about your program and release forms for photographs and children's work samples.

Chapter 1

Why Use Portfolios?

You are probably reading this book for one or more of the following reasons:

- you are wondering just what portfolios are and how you can use them in your classroom;

- you want to improve your teaching and help children learn more effectively;

- a friend or colleague has told you that portfolios have transformed his classroom into a wonderful place where children (and teachers) are thinking and discussing and writing and learning all of the time;

- you have noticed all of the attention to portfolios in early childhood journals, resource catalogs and conference programs, and you are wondering what it's all about;

- you are troubled by the emphasis on standardized testing of young children and you want to focus on individualized assessment instead; and

- your child care program or school is under orders from above to "do portfolios" and you need to get up to speed quickly.

Whatever your reason, we're glad you picked up our book. We think you'll find our ten-step portfolio process clear and feasible for preschool and primary classrooms. You can implement our process one step at a time and know that you are making progress. Why is our process achievable? The answer is simple: it lets you proceed at your own pace; it shows you how to become a better, more effective teacher; and it focuses on finding out how young children are different, rather than proving how they are the same.

In *The Portfolio Book*, we present a relatively simple process for using portfolios to support improved learning for children, teachers and families. Our idea is to use portfolios for their original purpose, to encourage reflection and goal-setting by individual learners and to engage parents in assessment and evaluation through frequent and varied *communication*. In this book, we concentrate on the many ways in which individual teachers and the children in their classes can learn more through the use of portfolios. The ten-step portfolio process is designed to permit teachers and administrators to implement portfolios gradually. You can start with a single, small step and complete the process over two or three school years.

The Portfolio Book

The ten-step portfolio process supports:

- Individualized instruction for young children within the context of broad learning goals,

- Continuous professional development by teachers and caregivers, and

- Rich family involvement in the early childhood program.

Getting Over the Hurdle of Written Records

One of the ways the ten-step portfolio process makes all of this possible is because it helps professionals over the hurdle that throws many of us: *written records*. Thousands of early childhood teachers and caregivers, wanting to use portfolios in their programs, have enthusiastically begun collecting work samples and even photographing young learners in action, but many have lost steam at writing anecdotal and systematic records and narrative reports. This has been true even though there is wide agreement on the value of such written records as evidence of the teacher's unique perspective and insights and the child's unique interests, strengths and needs.

Why has the process of keeping written records stopped so many early childhood professionals in their tracks? One reason is that many teachers and school administrators consider teaching, on the one hand, and assessment and evaluation, on the other hand, to be separate educational activities. Written records are time-consuming and teachers don't want to spend "too much time" on assessment. Yet we cannot really separate these processes! Assessment, evaluation and teaching are part of one continuous cycle of teaching and learning.

Anecdotal Records

We simplify all of the writing tasks of portfolio-based assessment by breaking them down. We will lead you along a series of practical steps that will give you lots of practice at observing your students and keeping written records. By the time you reach anecdotal records (Step Seven) and narrative reports (Step Eight) in the ten-step portfolio process, you will be ready. As an added benefit, your expanding skills as a writer will make you a better teacher of young writers.

This chapter of *The Portfolio Book* gives you some background information on assessment and evaluation. In Chapter Two, we will summarize how portfolios support child-centered learning and developmentally appropriate practice in early childhood education and care. In Chapter Three we describe what you can do to get ready to implement the ten-step portfolio process, and in Chapter Four we outline a typical portfolio and its contents. Then, in Chapter Five, we guide you through the ten-step portfolio process, showing how each step supports family participation and discussing how that involvement can make teachers and parents stronger allies. We show how portfolio-based assessment is a process of innovation and adaptation, with teachers and caregivers testing and revising new techniques. Throughout the process, teachers become more skillful and insightful, children learn more effectively and parents become even more involved in their children's development.

There is nothing magical about the ten-step portfolio process, but it is easier than many portfolio systems. Those systems often include numerous complicated forms for systematically recording information about children's mastery of discrete skills and concepts. We believe that simpler devices, such as learning logs, anecdotal records and interviews, can enable teachers and children to record important information and set new learning goals and objectives on the basis of that information. Moreover, these easy techniques enable you to incorporate portfolios into the everyday life of the classroom. Your classroom portfolios can become an essential aspect of the learning community, not just another "add-on."

After you are comfortable with our simple techniques, you may want to incorporate record-keeping strategies from other systems. However, we believe that our system is sufficient for supporting a learning community. Standard forms and performance tasks may allow for system-wide comparisons, but they will not provide the same richness or depth of information about individual children.

Portfolios Support Child-Centered Learning

Portfolio-based assessment can and should focus everyone's attention—children's, teachers' and family members'—on the important tasks of learning. The process can stimulate questioning, discussing, guessing, proposing, analyzing and reflecting. The portfolio strategies that we suggest in this book are light on paperwork and light on standardized measurements, but heavy on learning for teachers, children and parents. These ideas support the child-centered approach to curriculum and instruction that many of us know as the "project approach." Through one-on-one interviews with individual children, as well as through regular observations of children, teachers and caregivers can discover the topics and questions that excite children and motivate them to investigate and experiment.

The Portfolio Book

The Ten-Step Portfolio Process

1. Establish a Portfolio Policy

2. Collect Work Samples

3. Take Photographs

4. Use Learning Logs

5. Interview Children

6. Take Systematic Records

7. Take Anecdotal Records

8. Prepare Narrative Reports

9. Conduct Three-way Portfolio Conferences

10. Prepare Pass-along Portfolios

We have broken the process of implementing portfolios into ten simple steps. As you master each of the steps, you may want to combine one with another. For example, as learning log conferences lead to interviews, you may want to dispense with separate learning log conferences with some children, but find that they remain useful in helping other children keep track of tasks and goals. All children will not develop the capacity for reflection about their work at the same rate, so the structure of learning log conferences will be more valuable to some. Likewise, anecdotal records may be more valuable as you assess children who do not respond well in the interview situation. These portfolio techniques are flexible to enable you to adapt your assessment strategies according to the needs of individual children.

Implement The Ten-Step Process Gradually

The ten-step portfolio process is designed to permit teachers, caregivers and administrators to implement portfolios gradually. You can start with a single, small step and complete the process over two or three school years, or you can implement the ten-step process over one school year. We start with establishment of a portfolio policy, an essential step that many programs, in the rush to "do portfolios," unfortunately skip. From there, we move to the simplest, most common portfolio strategy: collection of work samples. Then our process for portfolio implementation guides the early childhood practitioner to the final, best and highest use of portfolios, in three-way portfolio conferences (conferences with parents, child and teacher) and as research material for narrative reports.

Learn to Plan More Effectively

The ten-step portfolio process will help you understand children's development better and plan learning activities more effectively. This professional focus on observation will also generate material for workshops, presentations, articles, action research—even books!

Involve Families

Our process has another distinctive feature. We emphasize that the portfolio can open the learning process to parents, siblings and extended family members—engaging them in the life of the classroom or center. In this way, the portfolio becomes a tool for family-centered curriculum development. Educators and parents who are already routinely communicating with families see this as an opportunity to develop a circle of learning that extends from school to home and back again. For those parents and teachers who are not engaged in routine communication with families, incorporating topics, materials and projects that are home- or family-based can initiate meaningful school-home communication.

Bradley had always been interested in merchandise and money. He mastered mathematical concepts easily and used math skills to think about things he might buy, sell or trade. Recognizing his serious interest in retail transactions, his mother arranged for the boy to work as an "apprentice" in a small bookstore. She paid the bookseller (in restaurant gift certificates) to allow the boy to hang around the store. The bookseller showed Bradley how he traded rare and used books. He explained the role of distributors in the book trade. He taught the boy

how to operate the cash register and the microfiche reader. He even assisted the boy in handling some credit card transactions with customers. Bradley learned a lot about the retail business. He was eight years old and in the third grade.

The same year, Bradley's "gifted and talented" teacher designed a unit on economics. She asked her class to design an imaginary business and conduct imaginary transactions. As a final project, individual children were to create "economic timelines" in the form of "shoe box televisions" or "timeline belts."

Bradley's mother mentioned her son's first-hand knowledge of retail business to the teacher, suggesting that Bradley could apply his knowledge during the unit on economics. But the teacher said that, unfortunately, the boy's experience working in a store did not fit into her plans for the unit. It would not be possible for him to share his knowledge with the class.

In a portfolio-based classroom, the teacher would have taken advantage of the mother's interest in supporting Bradley's learning. The teacher would have encouraged the boy to write about his experience as a bookseller's apprentice in a journal or learning log. The teacher would have recognized and respected his expertise and involved him in investigating the topic further in class. Meaningful portfolio-based assessment opens the doors between school or center and home, helping us make sure that we can build upon each child's and family's unique strengths and interests to support every child's full growth and development.

Reflection

We are not suggesting that the ten-step portfolio process is a substitute for wide-scale, standardized assessment. Portfolios cannot support that type of assessment without a huge amount of work by teachers and administrators. Graves (1992) suggests that portfolios are "simply too good an idea" to be limited to standardized collections of items for the purpose of comparing children to each other or to standards for achievement. We agree. Standardization of portfolios undermines the real benefit of portfolio-based assessment, which is as a framework or context for intimate, one-on-one, child-centered process learning. Unfortunately, where there is pressure for measurable data, portfolio assessment can emphasize tracking children's progress along narrow paths or on comparing children to each other. At the same time, we should work harder to educate parents about the benefits and limitations of different assessment strategies, so they will understand that a standardized test will not reveal anything new about their children, while a portfolio cannot tell them how their child compares to other children in the classroom, around the state or across the nation.

While other books about portfolios will tell you how to standardize, assess, evaluate and score portfolios themselves, we do not. Education in the United States already has systems for comparing children, classes, teachers, schools and school systems. We have report cards, standardized tests, accreditation and contests galore. We rank and sort and promote and reject learners every day of the year. Let's preserve portfolios as a foundation and context for learning, as records of individual children's unique experiences and accomplishments!

References

DeVries, R., and Kohlberg, L. (1987). *Constructivist Early Education: Overview and Comparison With Other Programs*. Washington, D.C.: National Association for the Education of Young Children. Cited in Burchfield, D. W. (1996). Teaching All Children: Developmentally Appropriate Curricular and Instructional Strategies in Primary-grade Classrooms. *Young Children* 52(1):4-10.

Graves, D. H. (1992). Portfolios: Keep a good idea growing. In Graves, D. H. and Sunstein, B. S., eds., *Portfolio Portraits*. Portsmouth, NH: Heinemann, 1.

Graves, D. H., and Sunstein, B. S., eds. (1992). *Portfolio Portraits*. Portsmouth, NH: Heinemann.

Katz, L. G., and Chard, S. C. (1989). *Engaging Children's Minds: The Project Approach*. Norwood, NJ: Ablex.

Segar, F. D. (1992). Portfolio definitions: Toward a shared notion. In Graves, D. H., and Sunstein, B. S., eds., *Portfolio Portraits*. Portsmouth, NH: Heinemann, 114-124.

Viadero, D. (1995). Even as Popularity Soars, Portfolios Encounter Roadblocks. *Education Week* 14(28).

To Learn More

Gardner, H. (1993). *Multiple Intelligences: The Theory in Practice; A Reader*. New York: Basic Books. (See Chapter 12, "Intelligences in Seven Phases," for a discussion of the roles of portfolios in assessment.)

Grosvenor, L. et al. (1993). *Student Portfolios*. Washington, D.C.: National Education Association.

Neill, M., Bursh, P., Schaeffere, B., Thall, C., Yohe, M., and Zappardino, P. (1995). *Implementing Performance Assessments: A Guide to Classroom, School and System Reform*. Cambridge, MA: The National Center for Fair and Open Testing.

Picus, L. O. (1994). *A Conceptual Framework for Analyzing the Costs of Alternative Assessment*. Los Angeles, CA: National Center for Research on Evaluation, Standards, and Student Testing. (CSE Technical Report 384. Available from CRESST, Graduate School of Education and Information Services, University of California, Los Angeles, Los Angeles, CA, 90024-1522.)

The Portfolio Book

Simmons, J. (1992). Portfolios for large-scale assessment. In Graves, D. H., and Sunstein, B. S., eds., *Portfolio Portraits*. Portsmouth, NH: Heinemann, 97.

Tierney, R. J., Carter, M. A., and Desai, L. E. (1991). *Portfolio Assessment in the Reading-Writing Classroom*. Norwood, MA: Christopher-Gordon Publishers.

How Portfolios Support Child-Centered Learning

Because portfolios have the potential to reflect children's development in the social-emotional and physical domains as well as in academic areas, they support child-centered programming for young children. The ultimate goal of portfolio-based assessment, for most teachers and caregivers, is to support child-centered learning. The ten-step portfolio process can help you reach that goal by creating a structure for much more extensive reflection and communication by young children and their teachers, caregivers and parents.

Seven-year-old Rian has moved four times in six months. He frequently dictates entries about his newest home in his journal, and at his teacher's suggestion adds "Kinds of Homes" to a topic list in his portfolio. He subsequently writes a very personal essay about the kinds of homes that he has had. After some revising, Rian publishes the essay at the classroom publishing center.

The portfolio becomes a context where the child can think about ideas and knowledge that he acquires outside the classroom, enriching traditional classroom show-and-tell activities. Although rarely discussed, this connection between school life and the private life of the child is as important as other home-school connections. The child also can think about her own progress and make decisions about what to learn next. This kind of self-evaluation and independent decision-making is critical to child-centered learning. Fully implemented portfolio-based assessment encourages children to reflect upon their own work, thus making the powerful connections between topics (such as animals) and experiences (such as observing the life cycle of a frog) that are the foundation of intellectual and creative activity.

Children who are experienced at reflecting on all of their experiences, examining their own work samples and thinking about their progress as researchers, writers, experimenters and artists gradually learn to set learning goals themselves. Of course, most children do not gain this important kind of experience without guidance and practice. Steps four and nine in the ten-step portfolio process create the classroom conditions for self-evaluation and goal-setting. Often, children's goals can influence the curriculum. If several children set the same or similar goals, you can plan a mini-lesson to provide skills or information that they will need. For example, if several children want to learn more about lizards after a zoo volunteer brings a lizard to the classroom, you might hold a session on "lizard research," showing them how to find the topic in an encyclopedia and in the library's card catalog or bringing books about lizards to the classroom and encouraging the children to write, dictate or draw what they learned from reading and looking at the books. You will have imbedded some research skills in a child-initiated project—and all from the input of children through the portfolio process.

What Do We Need to Know About Children?

The National Association for the Education of Young Children (NAEYC) identifies three kinds of information that are essential for planning appropriate learning experiences for young children: knowledge of individual children, knowledge of child development and knowledge of diversity, i.e., children's social and cultural backgrounds. We will explain in this chapter how portfolio-based assessment yields information in each of these categories, beginning with the needs of each individual child in the group.

Knowledge of Individual Children

Portfolios provide a structure for a variety of one-on-one encounters with young children and their families. These events in the child care center, family child care home, preschool, kindergarten or primary classroom are opportunities to learn more about how children learn as well as their unique abilities, interests and needs. With each encounter, you add to your knowledge about individual children, and thus to your ability to make informed plans and decisions.

By following the portfolio process described in this book, you will gradually strengthen your relationships with individual children and their families, in keeping with the NAEYC guideline to know each child well. Observing, knowing and understanding individual children is the basis of effective teaching, assessment and evaluation, and even family involvement. All of the steps in the portfolio process will help you learn about individual children's unique needs and strengths, enabling you to build upon the knowledge you constructed and fostering greater continuity of care for young children and their families.

Portfolio-based assessment can help teachers make adaptations for individual children, even in conventional textbook-driven, teacher-directed primary classrooms. The benefits of portfolios are much greater, however, where caregivers and teachers engage children and families in genuine learning communities. In these situations, portfolios become reference points for children and families, holders of developmental information and sources of inspiration and reassurance for learners who are temporarily discouraged.

Knowledge of Child Development

A thorough grounding in early childhood development across the domains (social-emotional, physical and academic) is a fundamental requirement for competency in early childhood education and care. Of course, no caregiver or teacher knows everything about child development, family structure, cultural diversity, accommodations for special needs or even learning styles. This is why continuing education is critical for practitioners. Portfolios support ongoing professional development because they reveal so many rich and relevant topics for individual caregivers and teachers to investigate. How does this happen? In implementing portfolios, practitioners continually observe and evaluate events in the early childhood program:

Was this activity effective with all of the children?

Why did some children not respond to the activity?

Why is this child preoccupied with a particular activity, and how should I respond?

The more that the teacher or caregiver observes about the development of young children, the more she needs to understand. For example, recognizing that some children do not succeed in following oral instructions indicates that another form of directions should be incorporated into classroom routines. In turn, this conclusion should encourage the teacher to do some background reading on how children learn. Thus, observation leads to refining and experimenting with different teaching styles and further research. The rich documentation of classroom events that portfolio-based assessment provides is the raw material for such reflections.

Knowledge of Diversity

By focusing early childhood practice on the needs and strengths of individual children and engaging families, portfolios also encourage greater cultural diversity in the early childhood program and greater support for children with special needs. Portfolios foster a community of learners—a community that can and should include children and parents with different home languages, those with physical or learning disabilities, and those with different family structures, cultures or lifestyles. Effective family involvement automatically fosters cultural diversity in the early childhood program because families are all different. Even where the population is quite homogeneous in terms of ethnic background, income, religious affiliation or other characteristics, differences exist: in family structure, in hobbies and occupations, even in physical abilities.

Portfolio-based assessment goes beyond involving families to support and celebrate diversity among children in several ways. Portfolios virtually demand that we ask for children's perspectives, guaranteeing that learning communities will become more aware of and sensitive to differences in experiences, interests and opinions.

Learning style is an important aspect of diversity. Young children learn in many different ways, depending upon their language, cognitive style, gender, temperament and other factors. Portfolio-based assessment enables the teacher or caregiver to learn more about individual children's approach to learning. As observation becomes a regular activity, the caregiver or teacher makes more and more discoveries about what motivates individual children to learn, how they learn and how they can be effectively assessed. This makes portfolio-based assessment a valuable tool for genuine cultural diversity in early childhood programs.

In addition to child reflection and teacher observation, a third feature of portfolio-based assessment supports diversity. Collection of work samples, photographs of bulky or three-dimensional works and demonstrations, audio/ video recordings and other items enables children, teachers and parents to preserve evidence of different intelligences, including the linguistic, logical-mathematical, spatial, bodily-kinesthetic, musical, interpersonal, intrapersonal and naturalist intelligences. This also enables children to demonstrate their progress despite differences in home languages. Portfolio-based assessment also allows children options for demonstrating their mastery of core skills and concepts.

Family Involvement and The Ten-Step Portfolio Process

Young children grow and develop as members of families; therefore, effective early childhood education must engage parents and other family members. (Family structures vary and can include parents, grandparents, foster parents,

guardians, other adults and even older siblings who care about the child's growth and development. For simplicity, we usually refer to the wide variety of family members as "parents.") Family involvement in early childhood education has traditionally consisted of teacher-to-parent communication through verbal and written messages, with the formal parent-teacher conference being the foundation of family involvement strategies. Teachers' and caregivers' communications to parents range from an infant's sleep schedule to behavior issues to brief reports, to the form of alpha grades (in primary grades) of children's academic standing. These kinds of information are important for early childhood professionals to share with parents, but they are not adequate for full family involvement.

It is critical that teachers and caregivers involve parents as partners in the early childhood program. This means that we must explain and defend any changes that we make in how we teach and care for their children.

In other words, changes in assessment and instruction must involve profoundly different family engagement.

Communicating with Families

Fortunately, portfolios can be an invaluable tool in engaging families in school or center life for two reasons. First, good portfolios support the traditional strategy of teacher communication, both through written and verbal messages and during formal parent-teacher conferences. This book suggests numerous ways to use items in young children's portfolios in communicating with parents. Work samples, teacher observations and children's reflections are among the materials that can be shared with parents in different ways. It is very important to use a variety of strategies for engaging families, because no single strategy will work for every family. Some strategies will be more effective with parents who have limited English proficiency, limited literacy skills or just bad memories of their own school days.

Just as importantly, the portfolio process described in this book prepares teachers and children to conduct three-way conferences with parents that are profoundly richer and more meaningful than the traditional parent-teacher conference. The three-way portfolio conference is an important part of the overall system of assessment and family involvement. It guarantees that the teacher, the parent and the child will be able to discuss the child's total development several times a year without interruption.

Family-Centered Curriculum Development

Second, and to our minds more important for lasting assessment reform, portfolios support family-centered curriculum development. As the individual child becomes able to participate in guiding her own learning, so the parent has new opportunities to participate in curriculum development. Family-centered curricula offer families many different ways to participate in their young children's growth and development. Familiar, local topics provide varied opportunities for family involvement across the curriculum, which can make them developmentally appropriate for young children and their families. When children's inquiries result in extended

The Portfolio Book

curriculum projects, opportunities for meaningful family participation abound. In this way, a community of learners flourishes and parents develop more confidence in teachers' practices. Family-centered curriculum is a significant step beyond the traditional methods of family involvement—and the ten-step portfolio process fosters the continual three-way communication among child, family and teacher that makes such curriculum possible.

• Implement portfolio-based assessment and instruction.

• Expand your family involvement efforts.

These are major goals. No caregiver or teacher can achieve these goals quickly. In fact, success in meeting goals of any kind requires identifying clear and achievable objectives and then establishing a timetable for accomplishing them. The portfolio process will allow you to implement portfolio-based assessment gradually and effectively. In the process you also can transform family involvement in your program so that parents understand, actively participate in and support the assessment and instruction of their children. This process includes numerous simple strategies for family involvement. Because families differ in their need for involvement and their ability to participate, effective centers and schools must provide numerous, varied opportunities for family participation. From displays of work samples, to sending home duplicate photographs of classroom activities, to inviting family members to join the class in a special project, this process incorporates family involvement extensively. Some techniques will support families with literacy, transportation or time constraints.

Each of the ten steps in the portfolio process (Chapter Five) includes a box labeled "Engage Families!" that contains simple suggestions for using your new portfolio skills to further involve families. Remember that good early childhood programs use a wide variety of family involvement strategies in order to engage all children's families. Some strategies will work for stay-at-home parents while others will be more practical for two-career households. Some of the ideas will meet the needs of very low-income families, while others may not. It is important to try as many different family involvement strategies as possible in order to engage every family.

Engage Families!

Portfolios can support a community of learners that includes family members in meaningful ways, particularly as members of the assessment team that evaluates individual children's progress and plans new learning activities to help meet specific goals. Portfolio-based family involvement can occur in three stages:

Stage One: Family members function as resources to the center or classroom, providing materials, information and volunteer support for investigations of topics selected by the teacher. As an example, after Janelle writes in her learning log about making a chair with her grandfather, the teacher invites the grandfather to demonstrate furniture-making in the classroom. The teacher has the greatest responsibility to recruit family members for this kind of participation. This is a step beyond the traditional family involvement strategy of informing parents of children's progress, but does not involve parents or other family members as partners.

Stage Two: Family members participate in planning units on local history, local ecology, local artists, local government or other topics. A teacher might observe during center time that several children are discussing a recent flood in the neighborhood of the school. She contacts a parent who is knowledgeable about the flood to ask for help in planning some lessons about flooding. Teachers still bear the greater responsibility for recruiting family members to participate.

Stage Three: Parents become "student-curriculum brokers," actually identifying the topic and resources that best fit their children's learning needs at particular times. For example, a parent sends a note to Janelle's preschool teacher on the day that Janelle brings pictures of her puppy for show-and-tell, explaining that her daughter has become very interested in dogs. The parent asks that Janelle be allowed to tell the other children what she is learning about dogs. At this stage in the development of family-centered curriculum, the teacher is highly responsive to parents' suggestions, so she asks Janelle to summarize what she has learned in her learning log and then to tell the other children about her findings during a whole-group period. At this stage, the parent is a full partner in the ongoing assessment of the child's needs and interests.

Professional Development: How Portfolios Help Teachers Learn

Ongoing portfolio-based assessment can support improvement of the knowledge and skills that early childhood teachers and caregivers need. These include knowledge of child development, a wide variety of interview and observation skills, the ability to adapt learning environments to meet the needs of individual children, methods of child-centered curriculum development and techniques for involving families in their children's lives at the center or school and bring their lives at home into school.

The Portfolio Book

Why a Teaching Journal Is Important

Keeping your own teaching journal is one strategy for stimulating reflection and self-evaluation. A teaching journal can be a valuable component of portfolio-based assessment and of your own professional development, as it is a format for thinking about your observations each day, noting plans and preparations, and identifying issues as they emerge in your professional practice. Because a private teaching journal can also give you valuable practice at writing about events in the lives of children, it will help prepare you for the writing tasks in the portfolio process.

The Portfolio and Professional Development

The portfolio is also a context for professional development. Portfolios provide many strategies for action research and for answering questions about curriculum, instruction, behavior guidance, family involvement and other important issues. By focusing on the interests, progress and needs of individual children, the portfolio reshapes the classroom culture and curriculum toward developmentally appropriate practice. Portfolios can support several different developmentally appropriate curriculum models, including instruction targeted to multiple intelligences, the project approach, the workshop approach and a blend of reading instruction strategies.

Classroom Research

The very process of implementing portfolios is a type of action research or classroom research. As a teacher, you continually experiment with new methods of instruction, assessment and evaluation. Discovering the techniques that work best in your school or program will enhance the overall program effectiveness. In this way, portfolios support ongoing professional development and even program evaluation.

Fundamentally, portfolio-based assessment supports reflection and communication by all of the members of the learning community—children, teachers, caregivers, administrators and families.

Reflection

A preschool teacher used her journal to describe a foray for insects by four-year-old Matt and two-year-old Levi:

> *Matt and Levi were interested in our new field-study materials—bug "houses" and a new magnifying glass. They were ready to set out immediately, and I followed. Turning over logs . . . we found a ready supply of sow bugs, immature snails, worms, ants and spiders. All of the equipment was tried out! Later, Matt led Levi on a long expedition to gather caterpillars, in this case the equipment being scissors to clip the branches on which they rest and a plastic bucket to house them in.*

How do you think this teacher's journal-writing supported child-centered learning? What did she learn about Matt and Levi? Did her observation of the children lead her to any new ideas? What do you think the teacher might have done next?

Conclusion

The portfolio process that we describe in this book is as much a way of teaching children as a way of assessing children. While some performance tasks and/or child-initiated pieces may be scored according to established criteria, most of the items in the portfolio process serve the day-to-day learning of young children in a developmentally appropriate manner. In addition, they support the entire learning community, including teachers, other professionals and family members. This is why we say that the ten-step portfolio process leads to *practical assessment* and *family involvement*.

In the next chapter, we describe how you can prepare to begin the ten-step portfolio process.

References

Bredekamp, S., and Copple, C., eds. (1997). *Developmentally Appropriate Practice in Early Childhood Programs*. Rev. ed. Washington, D.C.: National Association for the Education of Young Children.

Gardner, H. (1991). *The Unschooled Mind: How Children Think and How Schools Should Teach*. New York: Basic Books.

Jaelitz. (1996). Insect love: A field journal. *Young Children* 51:31, 40.

Katz, L. G., and Chard, S. C. (1989). *Engaging Children's Minds: The Project Approach*. Norwood, NJ: Ablex.

To Learn More

Alberto, P. A., and Troutman, A. C. (1990). *Applied Behavior Analysis for Teachers*. 3d ed. Columbus, OH: Merrill.

Armstrong, T. (1994). *Multiple Intelligences in the Classroom*. Alexandria, VA: Association for Supervision and Curriculum Development.

Bredekamp, S., and Copple, C., eds. (1997). *Developmentally Appropriate Practice in Early Childhood Programs*. Rev. ed. Washington, D.C.: National Association for the Education of Young Children. (This new edition of NAEYC's widely known "green book" is a vital reference for caregivers, teachers, administrators and parents. It possesses the spirit of portfolios, as the following quotation

The Portfolio Book

(p. 21) demonstrates: "[A]ssessment of young children relies heavily on the results of observations of children's development, descriptive data, collections of representative work by children, and demonstrated performance during authentic, not contrived, activities. Input from families as well as children's evaluations of their own work are part of the overall assessment strategy.")

Burchfield, D. W. (1996). Teaching all children: Developmentally appropriate curricular and instructional strategies in primary-grade classrooms. *Young Children* 52(1):4-10.

Comer, J. P. (1992). Educational accountability: A shared responsibility between parents and schools. *Stanford Law and Policy Review* 4:113-122.

Diffily, D., and Morrison, K., eds. (1997). *Family-friendly Communication for Early Childhood Programs*. Washington, D.C.: National Association for the Education of Young Children. (Reproducible information sheets about common concerns such as biting and the role of play.)

Duff, R. E., Brown, M. H., and Van Scoy, I. J. (1995). Reflection and self-evaluation: Keys to professional development. *Young Children* 50(4):81-88.

Evans, P. M. (1994). Getting beyond chewing gum and book covers. *Education Week* 14(7):44, 34.

Gardner, H. (1983). *Frames of Mind: The Theory of Multiple Intelligences*. New York: Basic Books.

Genishi, C., ed. (1992). *Ways of Assessing Children and Curriculum: Stories of Early Childhood Practice*. New York: Teachers College Press.

Graves, D. H., and Sunstein, B. S., eds. (1992). *Portfolio Portraits*. Portsmouth, NH: Heinemann.

Jauch, S. R. (1996). My special grownup: A respectful piece of the diversity puzzle. *Young Children* 51(4):73.

Kagan, S. L., Moore, E., and Bredekamp, S. (1995). *Reconsidering Children's Early Development and Learning: Toward Common Views and Vocabulary*. Washington, D.C.: National Education Goals Panel.

Lewis, E. G. (1996). What mother? What father? *Young Children* 51(3):27.

Marzano, R. J., Pickering, D., and McTighe, J. (1993). *Assessing Student Outcomes: Performance Assessment Using the Dimensions of Learning Model*. Alexandria, VA: Association for Supervision and Curriculum Development.

National Association for the Education of Young Children. (1995). *Guidelines for Preparation of Early Childhood Professionals: Associate, Baccalaureate, and Advanced Levels. Washington, D.C.: National Association for the Education of Young Children*.

How
Portfolios
Support
Child-
Centered
Learning

National Association for the Education of Young Children. (1996). Responding to linguistic and cultural diversity; Recommendations for effective early childhood education. *Young Children* 51(2):4-12.

Neill, M., Bursch, P., Schaeffer, B., Thall, C., Yohe, M., and Zappardino, P. (1995). *Implementing Performance Assessments: A Guide to Classroom, School and System Reform.* Cambridge, MA: National Center for Fair and Open Testing.

Puckett, M. B., and Black, J. K. (1994). *Authentic Assessment of the Young Child: Celebrating Development and Learning.* New York: Merrill.

Ramsey, P. G. (1995). Research in review: Growing up with the contradictions of race and class. *Young Children* 50(6):18-22

Shores, E. F. (1995). Interview. Howard Gardner on the eighth intelligence: Seeing the natural world. *Dimensions of Early Childhood* 23(4):5-7.

Simmons, J. (1992). Portfolios for large-scale assessment. In Graves, D. H., and Sunstein, B. S., eds., *Portfolio Portraits.* Portsmouth, NH: Heinemann, 97.

Spaggiari, S. (1993). The community-teacher partnership in the governance of the schools. In Edwards, C., Gandini, L., and Forman, G., eds., *The Hundred Languages of Children: The Reggio Emilia Approach to Early Childhood Education.* Norwood, NJ: Ablex, 91-101.

Tierney, R. J., Carter, M. A., and Desai, L. E. (1991). *Portfolio Assessment in the Reading-writing Classroom.* Norwood, MA: Christopher-Gordon Publishers.

Yinger, J. and Blaszka, S. (1995). A year of journaling; A year of building with young children. *Young Children* 51(1):15-19.

Chapter 3

Get Ready!

There are several ways in which you can prepare to begin the ten-step portfolio process. In this chapter, we will give you several ideas to think about. There is no single reason for beginning to use portfolios, and several different techniques can be good starting points.

An elementary school principal invites her faculty to join a discussion group on portfolios, giving every teacher the opportunity to experiment with portfolios in different ways. Seven teachers, out of a faculty of twenty-five, accept the invitation. One teacher decides to reform her science instruction through hands-on lessons and then asks herself what portfolio strategy would best serve that goal. Second-grade teachers at the school want to learn what their pupils experience during recess and decide to take turns making anecdotal records of the children's activities on the playground. A kindergarten teacher chooses to photograph her children during center time as a way of recording the wide variety of learning activities that occur; her goal is to assess and evaluate the benefits of center time for the children.

The teachers in this scenario take different steps in implementing portfolios. The items in their children's portfolios will differ. In every case, they take a step toward assessment that is richer, deeper and more meaningful than traditional tests and textbook assignments.

You can begin to use portfolios at any time. You may want to master just one or two techniques during your first year of using portfolios. As you take additional steps in the implementation process, you will be able to learn more about the needs and progress of individual children. With each step you take, you will extend your assessment strategies deeper into the growth and learning of the children in your class. The portfolios will reveal more and more information about individual children's progress—and about the effectiveness of your classroom practices. In time, you may even want to collaborate with teachers in planning streamlined "pass-along" portfolios that contain key pieces of evidence about individual children. You may want to adopt or adapt some strategies developed by other programs, or even components of commercial portfolio systems. At each step in the ten-step portfolio process, we encourage you to think about what you need to assess and how that step can help you meet that goal.

The Portfolio Book

This process is designed to simplify implementation of portfolio-based assessment and to focus on reflection and communication by learners, teachers and families. The pulse of early childhood education is the constant give-and-take between teachers, learners and families—communication that encourages reflecting on what has happened, involving everyone and arriving at common goals. We have mapped a portfolio path that leads to greater family engagement, more reflection by children and continuous professional development for teachers and caregivers.

Preparing

The sequence of the steps in the portfolio process is designed to lead you through progressively more involved tasks. While the sequence makes sense to us, based on our experience, you may wish to change the order in which you implement the steps. But we recommend that you do not rush into involving children and parents in evaluation of entire portfolios (step nine).

This process allows you to implement portfolio-based assessment in phases. Some teachers begin to implement portfolios with a small group rather than an entire class. We think this strategy may be helpful as you begin to make systematic records, but in general the steps in this model can be applied to entire classes at once.

If we compare the early childhood portfolio to a house, and work samples and photographs are the windows of the house, then written records are the foundation. Making written records for early childhood portfolios is a lot like being a newspaper reporter. You must make notes of what you find out and then present your findings in a form that is clear and useful for the reader, whether that reader is a parent, administrator or the child's next teacher. If you break down the task of writing about the life of your family child care home or classroom, the process is manageable. The ten-step portfolio process is designed so that you can gradually strengthen your writing skills.

Read a Lot

Give yourself a few minutes for professional and personal reading each day. Read articles or books about early childhood education, but read for fun, too. Branch out and try children's picture books, newspapers and magazines. As you read, ask yourself, "Is this telling me what I want or need to know? Have I read other articles or books that were better or worse than this?" Pay attention to the organization and style of magazine articles. Are there subheadings? Does the author present his or her main idea more than once? Is his or her tone friendly or authoritative?

Throughout this book, we recommend excellent books and articles about different aspects of early childhood education and care. Look for them in your local public or university library. If they are not available, ask a librarian about interlibrary loans. Your librarian may be able to obtain the items from other libraries and notify you when they arrive. You can borrow almost any book or magazine article from almost any library in the country—usually at no charge.

Start Writing

- Keep a *personal journal* about your hobby or family. In the beginning, use familiar words and a few short, simple sentences. To practice editing your own writing, review the previous day's journal entry each day and revise it. Strike out the repetitive phrases. Add information or comments to make an entry more complete. Find a writing partner and swap journals regularly (by electronic mail if you both have it). Write responses to your writing partner's journal entries. Are they clear? Interesting? Do they answer all of your questions?

- Next write your own *reading responses*. Jot a short note to a sister or friend about a novel you enjoyed. Post your reactions to a recent professional article on the staff bulletin board.

- Begin a *teaching journal*. Think of it as writing messages to yourself: short, daily notes about what you are planning in the center or classroom, what worked and what did not work, and what you wonder. Stretch mentally! Ask yourself questions:

    I wonder why Adelia never goes to the listening center.

    Why do I have so much trouble keeping the kids' attention during whole-group time?

    Jason's mother always seems angry at me. What is going on?

Then think about how you can find the answers. Gathering information to answer those questions can be the beginning of portfolio-based assessment—a new type of assessment that meets your unique needs. If you have not been a prolific writer before, keeping a journal for your eyes only will prepare you for the task of keeping written records in children's portfolios.

We suggest that you use a three-ring binder or planner, any book that has ample space for making notations in numerous categories. Create sections for daily journal entries and "to do" lists. Keep your binder or planner handy so that you can quickly record ideas.

The Portfolio Book

Along with beginning a teaching journal, find a journal partner or mentor. Ask your mentor to read your journal regularly, perhaps once a week, and write responses. A good mentor will respond honestly to your journal entries, pointing out unclear writing and fuzzy thinking. This will help you grow as a writer and as a reflective practitioner. In time, your journal partner can serve as a portfolio partner, someone with whom you can talk regularly about these new assessment strategies and how they are working for you.

Keep a Teaching Journal

The best way to prepare for the ten-step portfolio process is by beginning to keep a teaching journal. By keeping your own private journal about how you work, you will get ready for portfolio-based assessment in two ways:

- *You will begin to reflect on how to support children's growth and learning.*

- *You will begin to write.*

As you will find, reflection is the heart of portfolio-based assessment: reflection by individual children about their own work and learning goals; reflection by parents and other family members about what their children are learning and doing; and reflection by you.

Writing is the central task of portfolio-based assessment. From labels on work samples to anecdotal records to narrative reports, the process involves writing throughout the day.

A teaching journal will help you acquire these skills. If you have ever kept a diary or are in the habit of writing personal letters to friends or relatives, you may be ready to start your journal. If not, you might use the following questions as your own personal writing prompts:

1. What seemed to be the most successful episode of the day?

2. Did any child have an "ah ha!" moment in my class today?

3. Did any child teach another child?

4. Did any children ask interesting questions that could lead to investigations or projects?

You might also select a particular child or small group to write about. Answer these questions:

1. What learning activity was effective with (David) today?

2. Did (David) demonstrate progress in a specific area today? If so, what activities, materials or interactions supported that progress?

3. Did (David) have any problems today?

Focusing in your teaching journal on a particular child or group will help prepare you for recording systematic observations.

Once you have established your teaching journal and are writing in it at least several times a week, you may want to ask another teacher or caregiver to read your journal and write comments to you. Ask your colleague:

1. Are my accounts of events in the classroom clear and complete?

2. Am I asking myself good questions about these events?

Involving Parents in Portfolio-based Assessment

By providing many opportunities for children, parents and teachers to communicate about what they are learning, portfolios support family-based curriculum development. Each step in the portfolio process involves the children and their parents in reflecting upon the work and in setting additional goals. We also emphasize the importance of involving parents and other family members at each step in your implementation of portfolio-based assessment. The key to successful assessment reform in early childhood education is to genuinely inform and involve parents in as many facets of classroom practice as possible.

When you begin to change assessment and evaluation, such as how you formally report children's progress to parents, it will be important to explain the changes to parents in advance. As you take each step in the portfolio process, you share the new technique with parents in a letter, newsletter article, presentation or other format. Parents should already know that you are expanding your repertoire of assessment techniques and working to understand more about their children's learning styles and needs. Some parents probably have examined their children's portfolios during visits to the classroom. We hope that you have already shared selected items from children's portfolios during traditional teacher-parent conferences. As you expand the number and type of items that you collect in portfolios, you will have more evidence to share with parents at traditional teacher-parent conferences. You can use the conferences to explain how the items help you understand their children's development.

Parents have found several formal instruments effective to use, including the Adaptive Behavior Scale for Infants and Early Childhood (Leland, Shoace, McElwain, and Christie, 1980), the Vineland Adaptive Behavior Scales (Sparrow, Balla, and Cicchetti, 1984), the Battelle Developmental Inventory (Newborg, Stock, Wnek, Guidubaldi, and Svinicki, 1984) and the Parent Inventory of Child Development in Nonschool Environments (Vincent et al., 1983). Any records of parental assessment should go in the children's private portfolios.

The Portfolio Book

Assessment at Home

You can involve parents by asking for their help in gathering information. Parents are essential resources in developmentally appropriate assessment of young children because they have the opportunity to conduct naturalistic assessment in the home and in many other situations that teachers and caregivers never witness. You can provide many kinds of instruments to parents for use in assessment at home. You may want to develop your own simple checklists of skills or dispositions, perhaps for use several times during the year.

Checklists for parents also may gently nudge parents toward providing more developmentally appropriate opportunities for play and learning at home. (See the following checklist, "How Do I Love Thee? Let Me Count the Ways," that can be copied and then shared with parents.)

How Do I Love Thee?
Let Me Count the Ways.

We play together.

I ask, "What can we do together?"

I follow my child's lead when we play.

I praise my child's creativity and good manners at play.

I do not criticize my child when we play.

I play with my child often.

We play outside and inside, in the car and on the bus, with toys and
with just our imaginations.

We talk together.

I talk with my child about what we are doing.

I talk with my child about what we see.

I ask my child what he or she thinks about things.

I use "thinking talk" when we are together. For example, I might say, "I better use the brake
because we're going down the hill!" or "It's after three o'clock. The mail carrier should be
here soon!" or "I wonder what will happen next in this story. Do you think the boy will find
his puppy?"

We read together.

I read my child's favorite books aloud often.

I sometimes mention characters and stories in our favorite books even when
we are not reading together.

I borrow books from the library or from friends and neighbors often.

We read different kinds of books: picture books, books of poems or songs, counting books
and even grown-up books about art or science.

We sometimes look things up in dictionaries, encyclopedias or other reference books.

I tell my child about the books and magazines I read for
my own enjoyment.

The Portfolio Book

A checklist of household items that support young children's learning, such as nesting pots or bowls, can help parents assess their homes as learning environments. (For fun, this checklist might take the form of a "Garage Sale Shopping List." Be creative! Send parents a flyer with the following list or your own version.)

Garage Sale Shopping List

The best "educational toys" are not expensive. Keep a look-out for toys and other materials that will expand the fun and learning your child can do at home.

Classic toys

Stacking cups

Blocks

Large beads

Dolls

Dress-up clothes (Don't forget hats and sunglasses!)

Household "junk"

Jar lids (for stacking, sorting and nesting)

Cardboard boxes of different sizes (for making toy houses or anything)

Plastic tubs

Spoons

Cups

Old magazines

Equipment

Measuring tapes

Outdoor thermometer

Binoculars

Magnifying glass

Eyedropper

Tweezers

Microscope

In this chapter, we have given you some ideas for preparing to implement portfolio-based assessment. Review these suggestions. Talk them over with a portfolio partner, if you have one. In the next chapter, Chapter Four, we will describe what typically goes into a portfolio, and then in Chapter Five we will lead you through the ten-step portfolio process, one practical, effective step at a time.

About the ten-step forms: We provide simple forms in the appendix for your use with several of the steps. The forms are not essential. You can develop your own forms or simply use blank paper for most of the written records in the ten-step portfolio process. However, the forms may be useful as you first practice a new assessment strategy. Duplicate the forms on a copying machine and store a supply of each in a handy location in your classroom. You may want to use different colors of paper to distinguish one form from another.

Reflection

Margaret M. Voss and Laurie Mansfield were colleagues at an elementary school. When Mansfield decided to begin implementing portfolios in order to better understand her first-graders' progress as writers, Voss, a teacher-researcher, became a regular observer in the classroom, visiting twice a week from February to May. She and Mansfield also talked regularly about the strategies that Mansfield was trying. Voss later described the experience of collegial reflection: "After most visits we talked briefly during her lunch break or later by phone. I tried to be more an observer than a participant, though I provided Laurie with a few materials to read, and when she asked me what I thought, I discussed things with her. I solicited her ideas rather than offering my own, or I suggested alternatives she might consider, for I wanted to see how her experiences in the classroom influenced her decisions. (Voss, 1992, p. 18)."

These two teachers shared observations during regular face-to-face meetings. How do you think that having a journal partner might enhance this type of professional growth? Can you think of a colleague who might become your partner? How would you manage the exchange of journals?

References

Turnbull, A. P., and Turnbull, H. R., eds. (1986). *Families, Professionals and Exceptionality: A Special Partnership*. Columbus, OH: Merrill.

Voss, M. M. (1992). Portfolios in first grade: A teacher's discoveries. In Graves, D. H., and Sunstein, B. S., eds., *Portfolio Portraits*. Portsmouth, NH: Heinemann.

The Portfolio Book

To Learn More

Clemmons, J., Laase, L., Cooper, D., Areglado, N., and Dill, M. (1993). *Portfolios in the Classroom: A Teacher's Sourcebook*. New York: Scholastic Professional Books. (A brief, useful summary of five elementary school educators' techniques for incorporating portfolios. This book includes reproducible forms.)

Gilbert, J. C. (1993). *Portfolio Resource Guide: Creating and Using Portfolios in the Classroom*. Ottawa, KS: The Writing Conference.

Linder, T. W. (1990). *Transdisciplinary Play-based Assessment: A Functional Approach to Working With Young Children*. Baltimore, MD: Paul H. Brookes Pub. Co.

Wiltz, N. W., and Fein, G. G. (1996). Evolution of a narrative curriculum: The contributions of Vivian Gussin Paley. *Young Children* 51(3):61-68.

Chapter 4

The Portfolio & Its Contents (What Are Portfolios?)

Everyone wants to know, "What goes in a portfolio?" Actually, no two portfolios are alike because children are all different and so their learning activities must be different. Likewise, no two teachers should create portfolios that are just alike, although they may use some of the same basic portfolio strategies. The best answer we can give you is: A portfolio is a collection of items that reveal different aspects of an individual child's growth and development over time.

You can begin these collections with a single type of item, such as work samples, and gradually expand the portfolios to include more kinds of items. This gives you time to test, adapt and master each new assessment strategy before moving on to another. The ten-step portfolio process allows you to experience each type of portfolio assessment and discover the strategies that will be most useful in your program.

In this chapter, we will explain the three types of portfolios and then introduce you to the variety of items that can be collected and preserved.

Types of Portfolios

The three types of portfolios are:

> The Private Portfolio
>
> The Learning Portfolio
>
> The Pass-along Portfolio

The first type of portfolio, the private portfolio, is one you probably already keep. The learning portfolio will encourage richer reflection and communication within your program and with parents; it will be the most fun and the most rewarding to implement. The pass-along portfolio is a condensed version of the first two. It will help future teachers and caregivers understand more about individual children.

The Portfolio Book

These three portfolios have overlapping but distinct functions. By dividing your records about individual children among these three portfolios, you maintain the confidentiality of sensitive information, provide constant access for children to projects in progress and insure that critical work samples are not accidentally lost.

The Private Portfolio

As a teacher or caregiver, you have always kept various written records about your children. Some of these, such as medical histories and parents' telephone numbers, are confidential. Confidentiality is also important as you collect additional types of written records. You will probably want to store anecdotal, systematic and running records, and notes from interviews with parents, separately from the children's learning portfolios. Although these records are not stored in the children's learning portfolios, they are an important part of portfolio-based assessment because they provide evidence of individual children's progress over time.

Each type of written record deepens or expands your knowledge of an individual child. However, it is important for us to note that decisions about placement or other matters concerning children should not be made on the basis of a single written record of any type.

Children's private portfolios should be stored in a secure drawer or cabinet to protect the privacy of children and their families.

The Learning Portfolio

This is the largest portfolio and the one that you and the children use most frequently. It can contain notes, drafts and preliminary drawings for projects in progress; recent work samples; and the child's learning log. Once you begin to conduct formal portfolio conferences with children, this is the file you and the child will consult. Expandable or accordion files are a good choice for learning portfolios because they are sturdy. Children can store them in individual cubbyholes or in an alphabetical row on a low shelf.

Remember: the learning portfolio is the child's collection.

The Pass-along Portfolio

Key work samples that demonstrate major advances or persistent problems go in the pass-along portfolio. In the beginning, you probably will select these samples, but children and eventually their parents also can choose items for the pass-along portfolio. Selected photographs and recordings and copies of your narrative reports also should go in this collection. You, the child or the parent can present the pass-along portfolio to the next teacher.

One benefit of pass-along portfolios is that children and future teachers can review their past work and find leads to new projects. For example, a kindergarten teacher may find topics for journal prompts in children's preschool portfolios. If Shanika's portfolio contains her drawing of a new baby brother, done the previous year, her teacher might suggest a drawing or dictated story to show how much the baby has grown. If narrative reports about Sam indicate a strong preference for the works of Stan and Jan Berenstain, Sam's second-grade teacher might suggest that he write a report about the entire series of "Berenstain Bears" books. (Let's abandon the attitude that it is "cheating" to use last year's work and encourage children to build upon their own foundations of knowledge and interests!)

As your program or school begins to use portfolios, it will be important to establish a clear policy about which kinds of items go in private files and which files are open for children to examine and use. You should also establish a written policy that the portfolios are the property of the children (or their parents or guardians) and designate when the pass-along portfolio will be turned over to the child.

About Electronic and Laser Disk Portfolios: Some innovators are creating storage systems for floppy disks and laser disks. Teachers and students can store many of the portfolio items we describe in this book on a disk for retrieval on a computer. These are interesting systems; however, the costs in money and time make digital portfolios impractical for most teachers and caregivers. Another issue is whether such a system makes the child's portfolio less accessible to parents. This book emphasizes simple, practical portfolio techniques that will increase family involvement, so we do not emphasize electronic systems for early childhood programs.

Items in the Portfolio

Creativity is the only limitation on the contents of children's portfolios. As you will see in the discussion to follow, the variety of items that you can collect and preserve to document children's development is wonderfully rich. For children, parents, teachers and caregivers, opening a well-done portfolio is like opening a treasure chest. Some items will bring a laugh or a smile, some items will spark memories and some items will inspire young learners (and their parents and teachers!) to try new tasks or retry old ones. All of the items will provide information about individual children's growth and development.

The most typical items are work samples; of these, drawings and writing samples are the most common. However, the portfolio becomes richer and more useful as other kinds of items are collected. In this section, we will discuss work samples along with learning logs, photographs, written records and audio and video recordings.

In deciding which items to collect in a portfolio, the teacher is like the curator of a museum. She needs a collections policy that is based on her research and teaching goals. Following such a policy, a curator of a museum on plantation agriculture will not accept a donation of Victorian furniture, no matter how well preserved the furniture is. For the early childhood teacher, the portfolio policy guides her decisions so that there is a clear purpose for each item in each portfolio. We will suggest a sample portfolio policy for early childhood portfolios in Chapter Five (see pages 86-87).

Work Samples

If the reflections of children, teachers and parents about learning are the heart of portfolio-based assessment, work samples are the backbone. Children's original drawings, writings and three-dimensional creations are hard evidence of their developing cognitive and creative abilities. Collected and evaluated over time, they reveal the children's progress. Judy Taylor, a first-grade teacher, describes reviewing a year's worth of work samples by a particular child who was "just about the poorest performer in the class . . . [A]s I looked again over the collected samples of his work, I could see definite growth. The more closely I looked and the more I called upon my understanding of the development of writing competence, the more dramatic his progress appeared" (1996, 39).

One of the many exciting benefits of portfolio-based collection and assessment is that it validates the caregiver or teacher who is already using developmentally appropriate practice and encourages others to begin! After all, you cannot collect authentic work samples unless children are actually doing original work, so collecting work samples propels your classroom beyond worksheets and look-alike craft projects.

In addition, collecting work samples preserves primary sources of information of children's progress. *Primary sources* are original, unaltered materials such as drawings, letters and unedited stories. By contrast, measurements and comparisons of children's learning, such as traditional tests, are *secondary sources*. They are someone's interpretation of children's learning, rather than actual evidence of the learning. To learn something new, researchers must find and interpret primary sources, so collecting work samples is a good early step in portfolio-based assessment. It enables the teacher to learn something new about an individual child's needs and interests.

In an early childhood program, work samples in a well-rounded portfolio will include artwork and pieces of dictation or writing that indicate the child's level of emerging literacy. Ideally, children sometimes will dictate or write about mathematical and scientific experiences, so some work samples will provide information about their learning in those areas. With older children, results of performance tasks such as math problems or scientific experiments also are valuable work samples.

Ideally, each of the following kinds of work samples should have brief teacher comments attached. Writing these comments is the first step toward keeping comprehensive written records, as we will describe in Chapter Five. By carefully examining work samples, you can identify evidence of developmental milestones and of practice, or mastery, of curricular goals.

Children's Artwork

Most preschool and kindergarten programs provide many opportunities for children to create drawings and other artwork. Samples of their works are obvious items for the early childhood portfolio. Primary-grade children typically have fewer chances to create original artwork, which is regrettable. Not only do they miss out on a tremendous avenue for interdisciplinary learning, but the teacher who does not incorporate daily art activities sacrifices rich possibilities for assessment. In fact, a shortage of artwork in a primary student's portfolio may reveal more about the inadequacy of the early childhood curriculum than about the child.

For most children, drawing skills progress from scribbling to representation in a predictable manner, although the rate of their progress varies significantly. Selected drawings can demonstrate an individual child's progress. Label these with the child's full name, the date and comments such as "Typical of Emily's prolific artwork at this time."

Preschool teachers collected these work samples to document the development of individual children's drawing skills.

In the first series of work samples, the child advances from the scribble stage to the preschematic stage over a period of fourteen months.

In the second series, the child shifts back and forth from scribbles to controlled scribbles for eight months before advancing to the preschematic stage. After eleven months, a drawing with a sun and flying bird demonstrates that she has reached the schematic stage.

Scribble Stage
November 15

The Portfolio Book

Controlled Scribble Stage, March 25

Preschematic Stage, January 30

Work samples courtesy of the Educational Research Center at Florida State University.

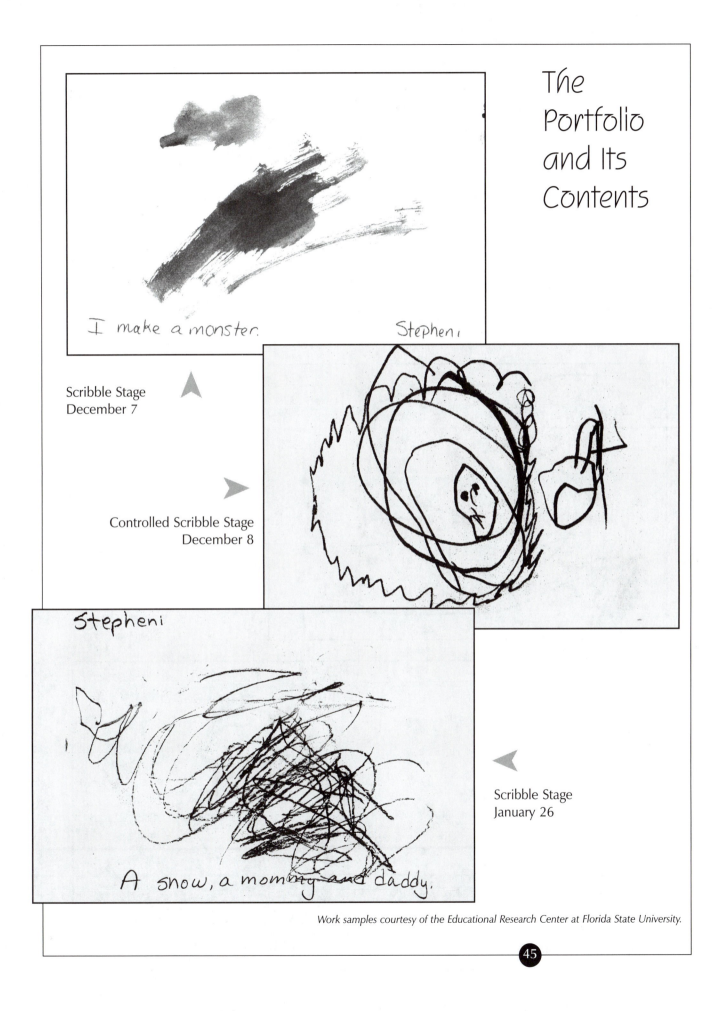

The Portfolio and Its Contents

I make a monster.

Stepheni

Scribble Stage
December 7

Controlled Scribble Stage
December 8

Stepheni

Scribble Stage
January 26

A snow, a mommy and daddy.

Work samples courtesy of the Educational Research Center at Florida State University.

45

The Portfolio Book

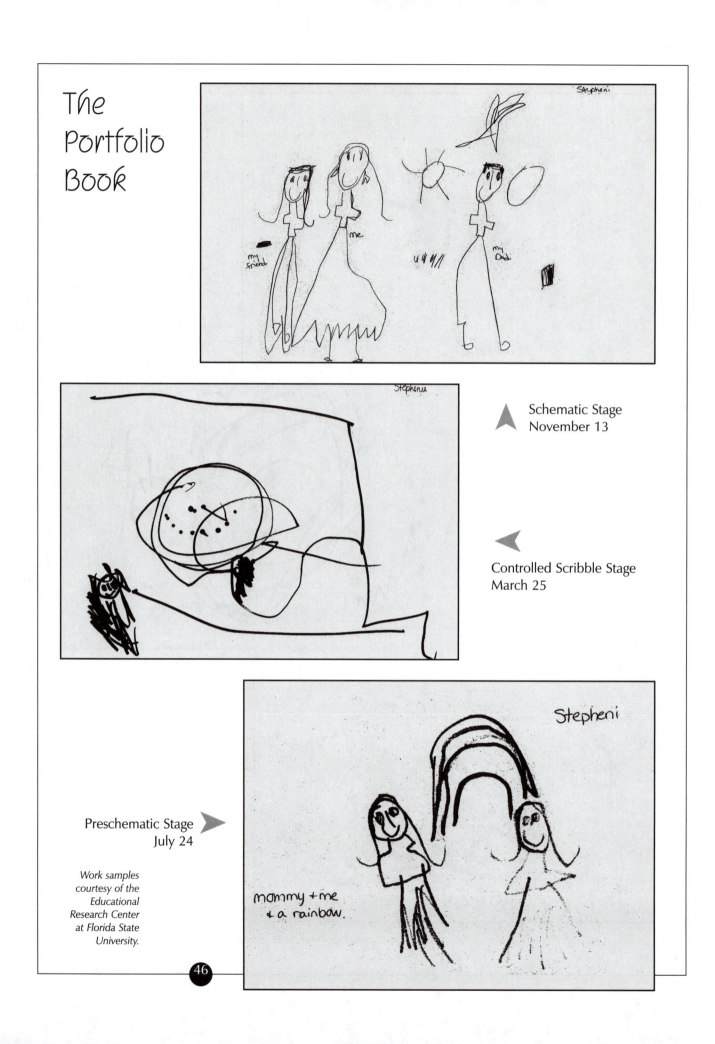

Schematic Stage
November 13

Controlled Scribble Stage
March 25

Preschematic Stage
July 24

Work samples courtesy of the Educational Research Center at Florida State University.

mommy + me + a rainbow.

Children's Dictation

Dictations are an important activity for the emerging writer because they demonstrate to the child the connections between play and narrative, and between oral and written language. They are an important type of work sample because they reveal children's ability to use expressive language. Narrative accounts of recent experiences and explanations of drawings or other products are useful in portfolios because they demonstrate children's thoughts, feelings and reflections.

Dictations should be collected repeatedly over time, and labeled with background information such as "Kelton provided this explanation of his sculpture" or "Kelton volunteered to dictate this story of his trip." Dictations may be saved in written form, on audio tapes or both ways.

A Bad Dream

I like to play. My mommy and daddy came to school on the first day of school. I was a little bit scared because I had a bad dream. I thought my teacher was going to be mean.

Work sample courtesy of Erika Rice and Carolyn Blome.

This new first-grader was invited to write and dictate sentences in her new journal about the experience of beginning first grade. She wrote two sentences herself. Then she dictated one additional sentence during each of two dictation sessions with different adults. The dictation process enabled Erika to broach the subject of her fears about beginning first grade. The sample reveals that during the second dictation session, Erika changed her mind about what she would add to the entry, revealing her emerging ability to revise her own writing.

The Portfolio Book

Writing Samples

Children's own writings are a third essential kind of work sample. A wide variety of items are appropriate for portfolios:

- Children's signatures

- Labels on drawings

- Letters to parents and others

- Journal entries

- Reports

- Original stories and books

▲ November 23

Drafts of writing are extremely valuable. Preserving early drafts serves two purposes. It demonstrates to the child (and the parent!) that revision is an important part of the writing process. It also preserves evidence of the child's individual writing process. This can be useful diagnostic information if the child needs extra support to improve as a writer.

This child's teacher preserved writing samples over a five-month period that dramatically demonstrate her progress as a writer during first grade. The teacher used the selected writing samples in her assessment and evaluation of Kelley's emerging literacy. Drawing on what she learned about Kelley's needs, she then planned what she would suggest Kelley refine, such as use of capital letters.

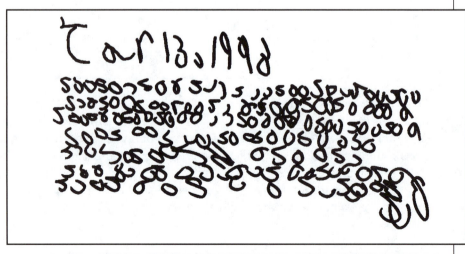

▶ January 13

> JaNl4 ls 1993
> Mi mom oed dad
> red to me ovr nit.
>
> mi mom oed dad like
> to red to me ova nit.
> we sit on the
> kab oed red, we
> oed WHAt A BAD
> DREAM THE
> SNOWY DAY my
> Brates the Book

◄ January 14

Work samples
courtesy of
Carolyn Blome

A note about children's journals: Many early childhood teachers now engage children in keeping journals. These notebooks or folders may contain children's responses to daily writing prompts, or they may be private diaries. We applaud the various interpretations of "journaling," but with a caution. Where children are encouraged to write their private thoughts and feelings, these journals should never be shared with others unless the child has agreed. This means that journal entries are not appropriate selections for teachers to add to portfolios unless the child agrees.

> Molr. 29, 1993
> I like my friends taye or nise
> I lik my friends taye like me
> I met tam at school taye
> ornise I like my friends
> my moma ndoaD like my friends

► March 29

Products of Performance Assessments

Performance tasks and performance projects are activities designed by the teacher or a curriculum specialist to assess children's mastery of specific learning objectives. These assessments are more common in primary programs than preschools. As a strategy for program evaluation, performance assessments can be an alternative, or a supplement, to mass standardized, criterion-referenced tests involving multiple choice and true/false questions. Good performance assessments reveal progress toward several objectives and are embedded in relevant, familiar curricular material. Performance assessments have the further advantage of being adaptable for different cultures. Writing prompts, dictated book reviews, demonstrations, experiments and small group activities, such as sorting objects according to two different criteria, are examples of performance assessments that are appropriate for primary-grade children. They can resemble routine classroom activities, making them less disruptive and stressful for young children. In fact, the tasks and projects can serve as learning experiences as well as assessments. Where performance tasks are included in portfolios, drafts and unsuccessful attempts can be as informative as final products.

Photographs

Photography is a powerful method of preserving and presenting information about what and how children are learning. Photographs remind the child of what she has done and help you report to the parent. Photographs also make it possible to preserve evidence of projects, such as group activities or three-dimensional works, that cannot be stored in portfolios. Of course, photography can be expensive. However, we strongly recommend that you take this step in spite of the cost. In the ten-step portfolio process, photography also has an important benefit: it is an intermediate step toward keeping written records.

Photographs are rich records of events. As a matter of fact, some historians specialize in examining old photographs for evidence about the past. They look for clues to when and where an event occurred and for details such as clothing or vegetation. Then they ask what the photographs signify about the scenes or events they capture. Classroom teachers use photography for similar reasons. Photographs capture the life of the classroom, especially when you are able to take candid pictures.

Photographs also can document individual children's progress over time:

> *"Kamisha reading her own writing aloud to another child for the first time on March 25."*

You (or a child) can repeatedly photograph a work in progress, to create a photographic record of how the piece was created. These photographs, along with candid snapshots of classroom scenes, can become fascinating material for exhibits about classroom activities.

The benefits are greater than this, however. Photography is important in the portfolio process for two additional reasons:

- Photographs help you practice observations.

- Photographs serve as writing prompts for making written records.

By keeping a loaded camera handy and watching for events that seem worth capturing on film, you will naturally pay closer attention to the meaningful hubbub of the classroom. Many events that earlier seemed insignificant will become more important when you ask yourself whether they are worth a photograph. You can use this same heightened awareness as you continually select or reject events to preserve in anecdotal records when it is not practical to take photographs.

As you gaze about the room, you notice Alicia and David have the water on at the sink. They are comparing the capacity of different containers by filling them with water and pouring it into other containers. You casually move close enough to listen to David and Alicia as they play at the sink. You hear Alicia observe that the short bottle holds more water than the tall one. Realizing that the children are discovering something about the properties of volume, you take the picture to record this learning moment. A quick snapshot and accompanying note will capture the information that Alicia and David chose to play with containers and investigate volume during choice time.

Photographs also will help you make those anecdotal records. At first, you may wait until the prints come back from the lab before you write your notes of what was happening in each event. As you examine the photographs and recall the events, you can write a short description of what was happening. You note when and where the event occurred because these facts demonstrate the benefits of your classroom schedule and layout. Writing these brief records during a leisurely examination of a new set of prints will give you confidence about what you write, how you construct the sentences and how much to write. Later, you can apply your new skill by making anecdotal records.

The Portfolio and Its Contents

◀

A playground shot documents six-year-old Willie's gross motor ability.

Photography courtesy of the authors.

The Portfolio Book

Stacking blocks
21 months

Symbolic play
2 years, 5 months

Catching a ball
3 years, 8 months

Photographs courtesy of
Susan Turner Purvis.

A second-grader holds her ceramic puppet for her teacher to photograph.

The Portfolio and Its Contents

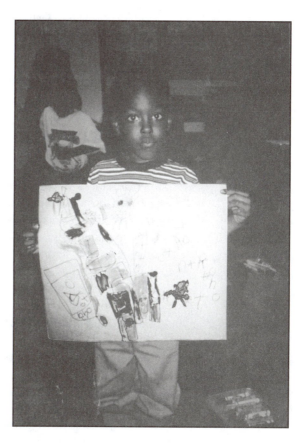

With a photograph, this child can save evidence of his oversized drawing.

This photograph records the activity of first building a block tower and then drawing it.

Photographs courtesy of Susan Turner Purvis.

The Portfolio Book

Learning Logs

A log is a record of performance. Ship logs are familiar to many people; the log is a particular kind of journal in which the ship captain makes daily records of progress along the maritime route. In many early childhood classrooms, reading logs are records of books that children have read. Each entry includes the title and author's name and perhaps some brief remarks by the child.

The short-range objective of implementing learning logs is to provide some individualization of curriculum planning. The learning log is a strategy for probing the individual child to discover new ways to engage him. The long-range objective is to enable children to set their own learning goals and plan their own learning activities.

The learning log is a variation of the typical reading book log. In a learning log children keep records—written, dictated, drawn—not only of books they have read (although that is very important) but also of events they observe, persons they meet, experiences they have. The learning log is similar to the journal, but different because it focuses the child's thoughts on what he has been learning—and what he would like to learn next.

The learning log includes the child's and family's learning experiences at home, at parents' work places, on vacation, etc. It can be an abbreviated record of everything the child learns, preserving facts and ideas discovered, books read, films and performances viewed, and even the things that the child wonders. The learning log is a useful tool for young children who are not yet readers and writers—it reflects all of the developmental domains. (In fact, the early childhood learning log can be thought of as an extension of the logs in which child care providers record events in the infant's or toddler's day, such as foods eaten and nap times.) Depending on your children's ages and the available materials, your learning logs can be a few sturdy blank pages stapled together, a series of dated learning log forms (copy appendix page 147) kept in a pocket folder or three-prong folder, a slender notebook or a cloth-bound blank book. Most children will substitute one format for another as they progress as writers. Whatever the format, the learning log should allow for written records of your one-on-one communication with the individual child about his or her learning progress.

One of the important reasons to introduce learning logs early in the ten-step portfolio process is that these logs will capture the kinds of learning that work samples may not. For example, you and the children can record their mathematical learning in a learning log. A second reason for implementing learning logs early in the process is that these portfolio items provide a structure for regular one-on-one conferences between teachers and children, supporting genuine relationships in which children can pose questions and form hypotheses with confidence. Thirdly, learning logs support emerging curriculum: learning log conferences can suggest topics for small-group or whole-group discussion. (Conversely, group discussions may also reveal subjects for one-on-one conversations.)

The children enjoy the funny story in a read-aloud book. Afterwards, during a short learning log conference with his teacher, Lorenzo comments on the intricate border around the book's cover illustration. He copies a section of the border in his learning log. His teacher invites him to find other books with borders in the reading center and compare them.

In our portfolio process, learning logs are a very important step for two reasons. First, they involve you and the individual child in brief discussions. Second, the learning log provides you with a regular opportunity to write brief comments about the child's ideas and interests, preparing you for keeping lengthier written records.

"Today you drew yourself wearing the glasses. I hope you will write a little next time. I always enjoy reading it.—Mrs. Purvis." March 14

"You made a nice picture of 'Chicken Little.' —Mrs. Purvis." May 16

The Portfolio Book

▶ April 18

today Jake We painted our crocodile We made ther another on Monday

"This is great 'Paper Talk' and so is your clay crocodile! Love, Mrs. Purvis." April 18

And I mad a Baby and eggs

"You're right! You were the only one in your class who made a 3-D puppet head.

Everyone else worked flat; they made relief sculptures.—Mrs. Purvis." March 11

today I made a rounded face. Everyone every one in the class made a round face except except me made Rarethe

Here Jake wrote exuberantly, emphasizing his enjoyment of drawing with a stick by repeating "very" five times. His teacher replied, "I'm glad you enjoyed drawing like Henri Matisse. You drew Richard (and you giggled a lot) and then put him in catcher's gear.—Mrs. Purvis." May 20

Jake used a second piece of paper to sketch the large drawing he had done that day. "Good sketch of your drawing.—Mrs. P." May 20

Work samples courtesy of Susan Turner Purvis

The Portfolio Book

Written Records

Frequent face-to-face, personal communication with parents, desirable though it is, might be difficult to accomplish. Written communication has to be the foundation for links between school and home. Through a variety of written records, portfolio-based assessment provides many ways for teachers, children and parents to communicate, even when one-on-one meetings are not possible. *Systematic records* are documentation of your planned observations of individual children—and therefore the documentation for many of your curriculum and instructional decisions. A series of *anecdotal records* is similar to a family scrapbook or photo album, a treasury of evidence about an individual child's development over time. *Portfolio conference summaries* preserve everyone's ideas about what the child is learning and can do. *Narrative reports* are comprehensive summaries of children's learning experiences, reflecting the teacher's perspective and the information derived from work samples, learning logs and other portfolio items.

By attaching short teacher comments to work samples, photographs and learning logs, you have already taken three important steps toward keeping comprehensive written records. If you have any doubts about your own ability as a writer, look at those written comments! You are writing! You also have already begun to adapt your schedule to allow time for making written records. You may have already found that this is time well-spent because of the information you are preserving and using.

In this section, we will introduce you to several other types of written records that complement brief teacher comments. We begin with interviews, which are extensions of brief learning log conferences and the bridge to portfolio conferences. For example, during a regular *learning log conference* with Jason, you may discuss the books he has read in the past week, the new shoes he is wearing and his ideas for playground games. Detecting an emerging interest in jokes, you schedule a time for an *interview*. Then you and Jason examine several joke books and discuss the kinds of jokes. Jason becomes inspired to create an original anthology of his favorite jokes. He stores this project in his learning portfolio and works on it sporadically. Still later, during a *portfolio conference*, you and Jason can review his progress and make plans to complete it.

Interviews

Interviews are the occasions when you and a child discuss a single topic in depth. Perhaps the topic is addition and you are assessing a child's understanding of addition and his ability to verbally express mathematical ideas. Or you may ask a child about a book she has examined. Your informal questions may lead her to dictate a reading reflection, her own commentary on the book. Interviews are opportunities for you to discuss information and ideas with children in a natural situation, while assessing their mastery of key concepts and skills.

Interviews may occur spontaneously during learning log conferences or center time, or you may plan to conduct them. Your notes of the interview preserve important information about what the child thinks and would like to know. Written notes of interviews enable you to keep track of individual children's needs and ensure that you will act on those needs as time allows.

You may occasionally record an interview on audio or video tape, particularly if there are developmental issues to be analyzed. For most purposes, however, handwritten notes of children's comments are all that you need.

The interview can serve as a qualitative pre-test or post-test of children's understandings. It is authentic because it embeds assessment of the individual child's knowledge in a genuine learning activity.

In the following example, seven-year-old Sam's teacher is curious about Sam's continuing difficulty with spelling in journal-writing. He sometimes substitutes "c" for "t," as in "cran" for "train" and "I climb cres today" for "I climb trees today." His teacher plans an interview to learn more about Sam's spelling, writing and reading. She takes notes as they talk and then types them up for future reference. Here is her record of the interview.

Sam (Age 7)

April 8

Ms. Suen: Sam, I'm interested in what you're learning as a speller and writer. Would you read to me from your journal?

Sam (reads from journal about family vacation): "We went on a mountain and we saw all of Oxford. I had English cream tea. I climbed trees today." (He reads more from his journal, reading most invented spelling with ease, but hesitates at some words, says "I'll skip that.")

Ms. Suen: That's a very good journal entry. I enjoyed learning about your trip. I noticed that you put "3" for "we" and then you had trouble reading that. Do you remember why you wrote "3"?

Sam: Not really. I was just writing fast.

Ms. Suen: And you wrote "cres" for "trees" and that mixed you up.

Sam: I don't know why I did that. Sometimes I make "c" s for "t" s.

Ms. Suen: You've been doing very well on spelling tests, though.

Sam: Spelling is my favorite thing at school.

Ms. Suen: Why is that?

Sam (sly smile): Because I can cast spells.

The Portfolio Book

Ms. Suen: That's a good one! You're very witty!

Sam: What??

Ms. Suen: Witty. That means you make good jokes. Do you enjoy making jokes?

Sam: Sometimes the whole class laughs.

Ms. Suen: What have you read lately that you like?

Sam (pulls book from his backpack): Mr. Brown Can Moo. Can You? (Reads entire book aloud, confidently. Hesitates at "rooster" and then identifies the word by the illustration of a rooster. Reads "how" for "oh" twice but corrects himself the first time. Reads "k-nock" for "knock" and then corrects himself.)

Ms. Suen: Excellent reading! What else have you been reading? Are you and your mom reading anything together at home?

Sam: We read part of Treasure Island *but it was too long. We read* Tennessee Boy.

Ms. Suen: What's that about?

Sam (sly smile): It's about a boy in Tennessee.

Systematic Records

These are brief, dated notes that you plan to make of specific incidents involving one or more children. You can use systematic observation to check the effectiveness of new lessons or center activities. This technique is also an unobtrusive way to document children's activities during an unfolding, child-initiated project, allowing you to record individual children's mastery of specific curricular objectives.

Kara mentions during a learning log conference that she has been watching the classroom pet turtles. She has noticed that sometimes the turtles stay half-submerged in the water and sometimes they crawl on the rocks and stretch their necks toward the window. Her teacher recognizes the opportunity to embed one of the school's science objectives, practicing scientific inquiry, in an authentic classroom activity. He speculates that the turtles may stretch toward the window to feel the sunshine. He suggests that Kara check the turtles at the same time each day and record their behavior along with whether windowsill conditions are sunny or cloudy. To document the effectiveness of this learning activity, the teacher reminds Kara at the appointed time on the following day and then observes and records her actions. To relate Kara's activities to overall instructional goals, he also notes the science objective. In this way, the teacher documents that Kara has met that objective.

The *diary description* is a variation of the systematic record. In this strategy, a teacher or caregiver regularly records observations of a single child, for the purpose of documenting changes in the child's behavior or interests over time.

Running records are another variation of systematic records. In this technique, you record a child's every action during a specific length of time, such as ten minutes. Running records require more time and concentration than other written records and, therefore, are difficult to make, particularly for classroom teachers. However, they can be useful when you need more information about an individual child's behavior or needs. After deciding that you need to assess a child's total behavior in a certain situation, you can ask a colleague or administrator to make a running record of the child while you continue your usual activities in the classroom. If you want to benefit from a "fresh pair of eyes," avoid sharing your hunches about the child when you ask a colleague to take the running record. For example, say "I'd like to know more about James' activities at the art center" rather than "I think James has some trouble with fine motor skills."

In the ten-step portfolio process, systematic observations begin as simple follow-ups to learning log conferences.

Systematic record sample

A preschool teacher decides to assess Anita's comprehension of a read-aloud story because her parents, who are new English-speakers themselves, are concerned about their daughter's mastery of English. The teacher plans to observe Anita during whole-group reading time and make notes of her responses. Systematic observation will give the teacher the information she needs to respond to the parents' concerns and intervene, if necessary. The systematic record is documentation of her observations in a simple form.

The teacher's notes:

Nov. 3

10 a.m. Whole group reading. Miss Coletta reads "Let's Be Enemies" aloud. Anita appears to listen closely. Says, "Brian always takes my crayons!" and "Natalie invited me to her birthday party." A. draws a picture showing her friends at school.

The teacher's comments:

Anita's comments during the story and her picture show that she clearly understood the language in the book "Let's Be Enemies" by Janice May Udry.

The Portfolio Book

Times when an aide, student teacher or volunteer is facilitating classroom activities are good opportunities to discreetly observe children. Frequent practice at systematic observation will prepare you to make anecdotal records, portfolio conference summaries and narrative reports.

Anecdotal Records

These are records of "child watching": your notes of the spontaneous actions of individual children, or perhaps of small groups of children. Anecdotal records are an important counterbalance to systematic records. While systematic records typically document children's progress toward predetermined goals, anecdotal records are authentic documentation of individual children's growth and development. They can capture the child's unique qualities. They are potentially the most powerful items in the early childhood portfolio, because they reflect your observations of events in the center or classroom—and you are the expert on everything that occurs in that setting! They are different from systematic notes because you do not plan to make them. Instead, you react to unexpected events by making notes.

When you begin to keep anecdotal records, you are truly functioning as a reporter in your own classroom, constantly alert to significant events and prepared to make accurate notes of them. Deposited in portfolios and regularly reviewed, these notes are clues to the needs and interests of individual children and further evidence of their progress in different developmental domains.

Anecdotal records are only as reliable as your observations. You must watch with an objective eye and be careful not to "slant" your notes of an incident. Yet a benefit of taking anecdotal records is that the process becomes a continuous, self-guided professional development activity. You learn more about child development, as well as the individual children under observation, every time you make notes about a spontaneous or unanticipated event in a child's day. This is especially true when you observe young children at play, when they are likely to use their developing language, cognitive, social-emotional and physical skills to the highest degree. With practice, you will be able to jot down anecdotal notes about particular children while you observe other children in order to make systematic records.

Anecdotal record-keeping can flow from photography in the early childhood program. Recognizing scenes worth preserving in photographs will give you practice at recognizing events that deserve anecdotal records.

In this example, a teacher snapped a Polaroid® picture of a four-year-old and his block construction and noted his explanation of the construction.

Anecdotal record sample

Oct. 22. Andre built a large structure—a museum for "stuffed animals, the real kind without blood." He then added dinosaurs and jungle animals and a few cars to drive around in.

Photograph and anecdotal record courtesy of the Educational Research Center at Florida State University.

The teacher later transferred the information to a weekly narrative report to his parents. (It would have been useful to explain in the narrative report that Andre's project demonstrated Stage Seven in the development of block play: "Children's buildings often reproduce or symbolize actual structures they know, and there is a strong impulse toward dramatic play around the block structures" (Hirsch, 1984).

Portfolio Conference Summaries

These written records preserve the ideas and insights that emerge during infrequent portfolio conferences. You can make brief notes during your conferences and then polish them into brief (one page or less) summaries a short time later.

While the interview focuses on a single topic in depth, such as the child's progress in compiling jokes or researching the life cycle of a caterpillar, the portfolio conference is a private conference concerning all of the child's learning experiences over a period of perhaps two or three months. (You may want to begin with two portfolio conferences per year and later increase them to three or four per year.) During the conference, you and the child (and eventually the child's parent or parents) spread out the contents of the learning portfolio and talk about them. The child may decide to return to unfinished projects or replicate a completed project in another form. You may decide to transfer a particular work sample, or a photocopy of it, to the pass-along portfolio because it demonstrates significant progress. At other times the child may choose to preserve a piece in the pass-along portfolio. (We think it is important to respect children's decisions regarding preservation of important pieces even when their importance is not clear to you.)

The portfolio conference is an extension of the interview, which is an extension of the learning log conference. In our model, you gradually broaden and deepen these conversations with individual children as you incorporate the portfolio process into more and more of the classroom routines. Eventually you can involve

The Portfolio Book

parents and guardians in some portfolio conferences, so that the conferences are three-way conversations about the child's body of recent work.

The written portfolio conference summary is simply your account of the topics, ideas and plans that you and the child discussed during the portfolio conference. During or after the portfolio conference, record these summaries on separate sheets or as entries in the child's learning log, where you and the child can refer to them later.

Portfolio conference summary sample

March 27. Lorenzo and I discussed things he has read and drawings he has made. He has enjoyed "101 Silly Summertime Jokes" and the copies of "Spider" magazine in the reading center. He liked the poem "Betty Bopper" by John Ciardi and the "knock knock" jokes he found in the magazines. We noticed that his favorite things to read are funny things.

Lorenzo still likes to draw very much. He has been practicing drawing "aliens" with eyes that pop up. Lorenzo only uses pencil for his alien drawings. He said he is more interested in perfecting the alien drawings than in coloring them with markers or colored pencils.

I commented that Lorenzo does not dictate or write very much in his journal or his learning log. I asked him to dictate or write once a day about something he has done and to tell at least two things that he liked or didn't like about the experience. I encouraged him to dictate or write down the names of stories, poems or books he reads in his learning log.

Ms. Fletcher

Narrative Reports

These are your periodic written reports of individual children's overall progress as well as your accommodations to their particular needs and strengths. In the early primary grades narrative reports may supplement traditional letter grade report cards or replace them, depending upon the policies of the school district.

In our model, the process of gradually implementing simpler types of written records should prepare you to write useful and informative narrative reports. You will become more confident about your writing skills as you write more frequently about children's progress. You also will have created a rich file of written information that is material for the narrative reports.

Narrative report sample

In these examples, a preschool teacher makes brief weekly narrative reports to parents. These narratives reflect the teacher's practice of making anecdotal records. They are an excellent form of communication to parents and should provide practice for periodic comprehensive narrative reports of the child's development across domains.

Dec. 8. Elly is doing well. She has been taking more time to fall asleep at naptime. She loves having something soft to sleep with. Elly started to sing "Oh, Christmas Tree" when we were talking about decorating Christmas trees.

Feb. 23. Elly has been talking a lot about Pocahontas. She can describe Pocahontas in detail. Elly has been trying to tie her own shoes. She can only get the laces wrapped together so far.

March 29. Elly has enjoyed playing with the other children. She played with the train with Andre and with the animals with McKinley. When she plays like that, she gets into some wonderful dramatic play.

Narrative reports courtesy of the Educational Research Center at Florida State University.

Audio and Video Recordings

Tape recordings are rich sources of information about children's learning. Moreover, we recommend them because they are especially valuable for family involvement, allowing parents with access to cassette players to see and hear events they otherwise would not experience. An audio recording of a child retelling a story, reading his own story aloud, practicing words in a foreign language or singing a song can be thrilling evidence of language development for the child, the teacher and the parent. Video recordings can be even more useful, particularly if you are interested in the activities of a group.

Checklists and Rating Scales

Checklists and rating scales of various skills and concepts are a common feature of early childhood portfolios. These instruments can be useful for quickly assessing and recording individual children's abilities in a particular developmental domain. Because checklists and rating scales require you to observe individual children and pay attention to their development over time, they can be useful "thinking prompts" for the teacher who is working to make her classroom more developmentally appropriate.

The Portfolio Book

The best checklists are ones that you create according to principles of child development and the goals of your program. The following lists of developmental changes in three-, four- and five-year-olds are from *Developmentally Appropriate Practice in Early Childhood Programs* (Bredekamp and Copple, 1997), the essential guide published by the National Association for the Education of Young Children. Use them to be sure that your curriculum is appropriate for preschoolers and kindergartners. The guide also includes a discussion of the wide variations in development that occur among six- to eight-year-olds and ways to link the primary curriculum, and assessment and evaluation, to their development. We believe the NAEYC guide is an essential foundation for portfolio-based assessment in early childhood programs, centers and schools.

Gross-Motor Development—Widely Held Expectations

For 3-year-olds

walks without watching feet; walks backward; runs at an even pace; turns and stops well

climbs stairs with alternating feet, using handrail for balance

jumps off low steps or objects; does not judge well in jumping over objects

shows improved coordination; begins to move legs and arms to pump a swing or ride a trike, sometimes forgetting to watch the direction of these actions and crashing into objects

perceives height and speed of objects (like a thrown ball) but may be overly bold or fearful, lacking a realistic sense of own ability

stands on one foot unsteadily; balances with difficulty on the low balance beam (four-inch width) and watches feet

plays actively (trying to keep up with older children) and then needs rest; fatigues suddenly and becomes cranky if overly tired

For 4-year-olds

walks heel-to-toes; skips unevenly; runs well

stands on one foot for five seconds or more; masters the low beam (four-inch width) but has difficulty on the two-inch beam without watching feet

walks down steps, alternating feet; judges well in placing feet on climbing structures

develops sufficient timing to jump rope or play games requiring quick reactions

begins to coordinate movements to climb on a jungle gym or jump on a small trampoline

shows greater perceptual judgment and awareness of own limitations and/or the consequences of unsafe behaviors; still needs supervision crossing a street or protecting self in certain activities

exhibits increased endurance, with long periods of high energy (needing increased intakes of liquids and calories); sometimes becomes overexcited and less self-regulated in group activities

For 5-year-olds

walks backward quickly; skips and turns with agility and speed; can incorporate motor skills into a game

walks a two-inch balance beam well, jumps over objects

hops well; maintains an even gate in stepping

jumps down several steps; jumps rope

climbs well; coordinates movements for swimming or bike riding

shows uneven perceptual judgment; acts overly confident at times but accepts limit setting and follows rules

displays high energy levels; rarely shows fatigue; finds inactivity difficult and seeks active games and environments

Fine-Motor Development—Widely Held Expectations

For 3-year-olds

places large pegs into pegboards; strings large beads; pours liquids with some spills

builds block towers; easily does puzzles with whole objects represented as a piece

fatigues easily if much hand coordination is required

draws shapes, such as the circle; begins to design objects, such as a house or figure; draws in some relation to each other

holds crayon or markers with fingers instead of the fist

undresses without assistance but needs help getting dressed; unbuttons skillfully but buttons slowly

For 4-year-olds

uses small pegs and board; strings small beads (and may do so in a pattern); pours sand and liquid into small containers

builds complex block structures that extend vertically; shows limited spatial judgment and tends to knock things over

enjoys manipulating play objects that have fine parts; likes to use scissors; practices an activity many times to gain mastery

draws combination of simple shapes; draws persons with at least four parts and objects that are recognizable to adults

dresses and undresses without adult assistance; brushes teeth and combs hair; spills rarely with cup or spoon; laces shoes or clothing but cannot yet tie

For 5-year-olds

hits nail with hammer head; uses scissors and screwdrivers unassisted

uses computer keyboard

builds three-dimensional block structures; does 10-15 piece puzzles with ease

likes to disassemble and reassemble objects and dress and undress dolls

has basic grasp of right and left but mixes them up at times

copies shapes; combines more than two geometric forms in drawing and construction

draws persons; prints letters crudely but most are recognizable by an adult; includes a context or scene in drawings; prints first name

zips coats; buttons well; ties shoes with adult coaching; dresses quickly

Language and Communication Development—Widely Held Expectations

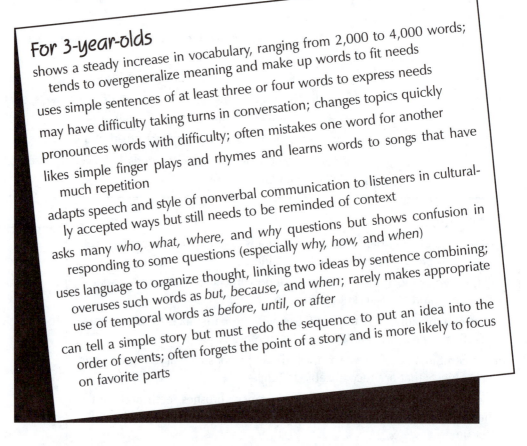

For 3-year-olds

shows a steady increase in vocabulary, ranging from 2,000 to 4,000 words; tends to overgeneralize meaning and make up words to fit needs

uses simple sentences of at least three or four words to express needs

may have difficulty taking turns in conversation; changes topics quickly

pronounces words with difficulty; often mistakes one word for another

likes simple finger plays and rhymes and learns words to songs that have much repetition

adapts speech and style of nonverbal communication to listeners in culturally accepted ways but still needs to be reminded of context

asks many *who, what, where,* and *why* questions but shows confusion in responding to some questions (especially *why, how,* and *when*)

uses language to organize thought, linking two ideas by sentence combining; overuses such words as *but, because,* and *when*; rarely makes appropriate use of temporal words as *before, until,* or *after*

can tell a simple story but must redo the sequence to put an idea into the order of events; often forgets the point of a story and is more likely to focus on favorite parts

For 4-year-olds

expands vocabulary from 4,000 to 6,000 words; shows more attention to abstract uses

likes to sing simple songs; knows many rhymes and finger plays

will talk in front of groups with some reticence; likes to tell others about family and experiences

uses verbal commands to claim many things; begins teasing others

expresses emotions through facial gestures and reads others for body cues; copies behaviors (such as hand gestures) of older children or adults

can control volume of voice for periods of time if reminded; begins to read context for social cues

uses more advanced sentence structure, such as relative clauses and tag questions ("She's nice, isn't she?") and experiments with new constructions, creating some comprehension difficulties for the listener

tries to communicate more than his or her vocabulary allows; borrows and extends words to create meaning

learns new vocabulary quickly if related to own experience ("We walk our dog on a belt. Oh yeah, it's a leash—we walk our dog on a leash")

can retell a four- or five-step directive or the sequence in a story

For 5-year-olds

employs a vocabulary of 5,000 to 8,000 words, with frequent plays on words; pronounces words with little difficulty, except for particular sounds, such as *l* and *th*

uses fuller, more complex sentences ("His turn is over, and it's my turn now")

takes turns in conversation, interrupts others less frequently; listens to another speaker if information is new and of interest; shows vestiges of egocentrism in speech, for instance, in assuming listener will understand what is meant (saying "He told me to do it" without any referents for the pronouns)

shares experiences verbally; knows the words to many songs

likes to act out others' roles, shows off in front of people or becomes unpredictably shy

remembers lines of simple poems and repeats full sentences and expression from others, including television shows and commercials

shows skill at using conventional modes of communication complete with pitch and inflection

uses nonverbal gestures, such as certain facial expressions in teasing peers

can tell and retell stories with practice; enjoys repeating stories, poems, and songs; enjoys acting out plays or stories

shows growing speech fluency in expressing ideas

The Portfolio Book

Social and Emotional Development—Widely Held Expectations

For 3-year-olds

depending in part on previous experience with peers, may look on from the sidelines or engage in parallel play until becoming more familiar with the other children, or may engage in associative play patterns (playing next to a peer, chatting and using toys but having separate individual intentions for behaviors)

shows difficulty taking turns and sharing objects, activity changing form often during a play period; lacks ability to solve problems well among peers; usually needs help to resolve a social situation if conflict occurs

plays well with others and responds positively if there are favorable conditions in terms of materials, space, and supervision (less likely to engage in prosocial behavior when any of these elements are lacking)

acts more cooperatively than does toddler and wants to please adults (may revert to toddler behavior of thumb sucking, pushing, hitting, crying if unhappy with the outcome of a social situation)

can follow simple requests; likes to be treated as an older child at times, but may still put objects in mouth that can be dangerous or wander off if not carefully supervised

expresses intense feelings, such as fear and affection; shows delightful, silly sense of humor

For 4-year-olds

still engages in associative play but begins true give-and-take, cooperative play

shows difficulty sharing—some more than others—but begins to understand turn taking and plays simple games in small groups

becomes angry easily if things don't go her or his way at times; now prefers to play with others most often; seeks to resolve negative interactions although lacking verbal skills to resolve all conflicts

begins to spontaneously offer things to others; wants to please friends; compliments others on new clothing or shoes; shows pleasure in having and being with friends

exhibits occasional outbursts of anger, but is learning that negative acts bring negative sanctions; quickly begins to justify an aggressive act ("He hit me first")

knows increasingly what self-regulation behaviors are expected but shows difficulty following through on a task or becomes easily sidetracked, forgetting what was asked unless reminded; likes to dress him or herself; gets own juice or snack; cleans up without constant supervision but unable to wait very long regardless of the promised outcome

shows greater ability to control intense feelings like fear or anger (no more temper tantrums); still needs adults to help him or her express or control feelings at times

For 5-year-olds

enjoys dramatic play with other children

cooperates well; forms small groups that may choose to exclude a peer

understands the power of rejecting others; verbally threatens to end friendships or select others ("You can't come to my birthday party!"); tends to be bossy with others, with too many leaders and not enough followers at times

enjoys others and can behave in a warm and empathetic manner; jokes and teases to gain attention

shows less physical aggression; more often uses verbal insult or threatens to hit someone

can follow requests; may lie rather than admit to not following procedures or rules; may be easily discouraged or encouraged

dresses and eats with minor supervision; reverts easily to young behaviors when group norms are less than appropriate

The developmental checklists presented appear in *Developmentally Appropriate Practice in Early Childhood Programs, Revised edition*, published in 1997 by the National Association for the Education of Young Children and edited by Sue Bredekamp and Carol Copple. The checklists are reprinted with permission of the National Association for the Education of Young Children (NAEYC).

The Six-Year-Old
Behavioral Characteristics

Physical

Good ocular pursuit

More aware of hand as tool

Sloppy; in a hurry; speed is a benchmark of six

Noisy in classroom

Falls backward out of chairs

Learning to distinguish left from right

Oral activity; chews pencils, bites fingernails, chews hair (teething)

Easily tires

Frequent illnesses

Enjoys out of doors; gym

Adaptive

Loves to ask questions

Likes new games; ideas

Loves to color; paint

Learns best through discovery

Enjoys process more than product

Tries more than can accomplish (eyes bigger than stomach)

Dramatic play elaborated

Cooperative play elaborated

Representative symbols more important

Spatial relationships and functional relationships better understood

Beginning understanding of past when tied closely to present

Beginning interest in skill and technique of its own sake

Language

Likes to "work"

Likes to explain things; quick to explain things

Show and tell is useful

Loves jokes and guessing games

Boisterous and enthusiastic language

Worrier; complainer

Anticipates closure in speech of others

Personal-Social

Wants to be first

Competitive; enthusiastic

Anxious to do well

Thrives on praise

Any failure is hard

Tremendous capacity for enjoyment

Likes surprises, treats

Wants to be good in school

Tends to be "poor sport"

Invents rules

Can be bossy, teasing

Critical of others

Easily upset when hurt

Sometimes dishonest

Friends are important (may have a best friend)

Transitions are difficult

School replaces home as most significant environmental influence

Classroom Implications

Six is the stage of "sorting out" of great drive and eagerness. There are many important classroom considerations.

Vision and Fine Motor Ability

Children should do little copy work from the blackboard. While they will comply if asked, this is a difficult task at this age.

Spacing and the ability to stay on the line are difficult and performed with great inconsistency.

Tracking ability now makes reading instruction manageable.

Gross Motor Ability

Teachers need to allow for a busy level of noise and activity in the classroom.

Teachers should expect high volume of products but low quality of completion. Children are proud of how much work they get done, but not too concerned with how it looks.

Teachers can sometimes encourage a slower pace to enhance quality.

Teachers should pay attention to how much children delight in the doing; especially the doing for themselves, whether it be academics, clean-up or snack. Children are ready for experiments with individuals and group responsibility.

Cognitive Growth

Games of all sorts are popular and useful at this age. Language games, poems, riddles, and songs delight and illuminate the young mind. Teaching through games produces learning patterns that take root in a way that work book learning usually does not.

This is an age of artistic explosion. Clay, paints, coloring, book making, weaving, dancing, singing are often all tried out for the first time with seriousness at this age. Children need to be made to feel that their attempts are valued, that there is no right or wrong way to approach an art medium. Risk taking at this age enhances later artistic expression and competence.

Children can begin to understand past events (history) when they are closely associated with the present. Teachers need to plan social studies content with an eye to the here and now. Field trips are immensely popular and productive when followed by representational activities such as experience stories and work in the blocks.

Personal-Social Behavior

Extreme behavior needs to be understood but not tolerated by the teacher. Tantrums, teasing, bossing, complaining, tattling are all ways sixes try out relationships with authority.

Teachers need to be extremely sensitive of the power of their words with children at this age. An ounce of praise may be all a child needs to get over a difficult situation; severe criticism can truly injure.

Teachers need to be aware to take the competitive edge off games as they employ them for learning. Sixes are highly competitive and can overdo the need to win and be first.

The Seven-Year-Old
Behavioral Characteristics

Physical
Visually myopic

Works with head down on desk

Pincer grasp at pencil point

Written work tidy and neat

Sometimes tense

Likes confined space

Personal-Social
Inwardized, withdrawn

Sometimes moody; depressed; sulking or shy

Touchy

"Nobody likes me"

Changeable feelings

Needs security, structure

Relies on teacher for help

Doesn't like to make mistakes or risk making them

Sensitive to others' feelings, but sometimes tattles

Conscientious; serious

Keeps a neat desk, room

Needs constant reinforcement

Doesn't relate well to more than one teacher

Strong likes and dislikes

Language
Good listener

Precise talker

Likes one-to-one conversation

Vocabulary development expands rapidly

Interested in meaning of words

Likes to send notes

Interested in all sorts of codes

Adaptive
Likes to review learning

Needs closure; must complete assignment

Likes to work slowly

Likes to work alone

Can classify spontaneously

Likes to be read to

Reflective ability growing

Erases constantly; wants perfect work

Likes to repeat tasks

Enjoys manipulatives

Wants to discover how things work; likes to take
things apart

Classroom Implications

Sevens are "inwardized," moody; like to work alone. The classroom teacher needs to be alert to this sensitive age.

Vision and Fine Motor Ability

Children's printing, drawing, number work tends to be small, if not microscopic. Children work with head down on desk, often hiding or closing one eye. Copying from the board can be harmful. Inappropriate time to introduce cursive handwriting.

Children will anchor printing to bottom line; find it difficult to fill up space.

Children work with pincer grasp at pencil point and find it difficult to relax their grip.

Gross Motor Level

Teachers can plan for quiet room, sustained, quiet work periods with little overflow behavior.

Children prefer board games to gym games. Playground games such as jump rope, 4 square, hopscotch become more popular than team or large group activities.

Cognitive Growth

Teachers need to pay attention to routine and the child's need for closure. Children want to finish the work they begin. Timed tests can be especially troublesome.

Children like to work by themselves or in two's. Memorization is a favored pursuit. Children enjoy codes, puzzles and other secrets.

Children want their work to be perfect. Classroom attention to products, proper display of work is entirely appropriate.

Children enjoy repeating tasks, reviewing assignment with the teacher; like to touch base frequently with the teacher.

Teachers can successfully employ "discovery" centers or projects; children are eager to find out how things work. Like to collect and classify.

Personal-Social Behavior

Teachers should expect frequent friendship shifts. Children work best in pairs or alone; will accept teacher seating assignment.

Change in schedule is upsetting; plan well for substitutes.

Teachers need to modulate seriousness of classroom for sevens with humor and games.

Communication with parents is often critical at this changeable age.

The Eight-Year-Old
Behavioral Characteristics

Physical

Growth slows

Body control improves

Becomes skillful in maneuvering his bike

Large muscle skills have improved greatly

Rapid development and skillful use of small muscles

Crafts and projects are completed carefully and capably

Language

Able to deal with exceptions to grammatical rules

Developing increasing complex understanding on syntax

Communication somewhat limited because of inability to take the role of another

Has difficulty effectively retelling a story because he omits crucial information

Personal-Social

Wants to win and play by set rules

Ideas about rules are still vague

Constrained by respect for adults and other children

Refuses to accept any change in rules

Feelings of adequacy depend largely on success in school

Becoming more independent and responsible

Adaptive

Thinking becomes more logical and systematic

Uses analogies to past experiences to deal with new experiences

Uses conservation, reversibility, classification to problem solve in concrete situations

Becoming much more responsible and independent

Classroom Implications

Vision and Fine Motor Ability

Children are probably now ready for writing in cursive script. Drawings enter the schematic stage, showing attention to design, balance, and perspective. Small muscle skills become consolidated and develop more rapidly.

Gross Motor Level

Active play should be focused on learning skills required in organized games and sports. Activities such as walking a balance beam, tag, relay races, enable children to gain increased skills in using and controlling large muscles.

Cognitive Growth

Children are able to reason logically as long as problems are within the realm of their direct experiences. Teachers should be aware that though children at this age are more logical, they still have difficulty accounting for complicated situation.

Information or concepts must be presented by the teacher in as many ways as possible to account for the varying individual focuses of children.

Children at this age learn best from concrete objects and by actually doing what it is they are learning about.

Personal-Social Behavior

Children's relationships with their peers increase in importance and intensity.

Teachers should involve children in group activities that will enable them to win acceptance, establish roles, and achieve prestige. As children interact with their teacher they are learning to relate emotionally to adults outside the home and slowly achieve independence of family. A teacher should encourage the eight-year-old to assume responsibilities such as going on errands and taking care of his personal needs.

Permission to include these developmental checklists was granted by the Mississippi Department of Education. The checklists are taken from *Developmental Instruction Strategies: Kindergarten Through Third Grade,* published in 1992 by the Mississippi Department of Education.

The Portfolio Book

Preparing checklists of cognitive, social-emotional and physical development, along with key concepts and skills in your program's curriculum framework, would be a good exercise for you and your colleagues. However, checklists and rating scales can easily come to dominate your curriculum, so that mastering a few disconnected skills and concepts becomes the major goal of the classroom. When this happens, you have sacrificed the depth and the child-centered, independent learning that is the spirit of genuine portfolio-based assessment. For this reason, we do not emphasize checklists or rating scales as portfolio strategies. If you must use such instruments to record children's progress, then back up those check marks with narrative reports. Use the checklists as references for the reports, to be sure that you do not overlook any important developmental or curricular questions as you summarize an individual child's progress for a parent, colleague or administrator.

Storage

Storage is another common question. "What does all of that stuff go in?" Again, there is no single answer. Instead, you make this decision on the basis of what storage system you have in place and your personal preferences. You may use file folders, file pockets, accordion files, three-prong folders or even cardboard pizza boxes for most of the items. As you begin to implement portfolio-based assessment, your portfolios will probably be simple file pockets or large manila envelopes. When portfolios are fully implemented, however, assessment material is unlikely to fit in a single container. The receptacles should be sturdy and easy to label. Learning portfolios should be large enough to hold a lot of work samples; the private portfolios and pass-along portfolios can be simple file folders.

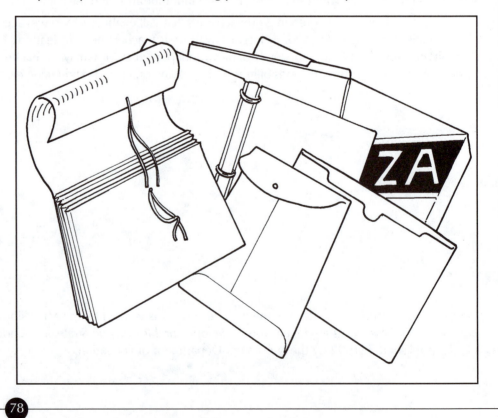

In time, as you implement additional assessment techniques such as audio or video recording, you will create assessment material that does not fit in a folder or pizza box. This is not a problem! You can store videotapes near the television set and audiotapes with the cassette recorder. In fact, portfolios can eventually enliven every corner of your classroom. Store the learning portfolios that children continually update and review on a low shelf. Keep date stamps handy at the art and writing centers so that children can quickly date their work samples. Look at the new batch of photographs in your in-box; they are ready for children to sort and add to portfolios and to the bulletin board in the hall. In the television corner, children watch videotapes of their own story reenactments. Private portfolios with medical information, your narrative reports and other confidential material are in a drawer of your desk.

Putting It All Together

In this chapter, we have described three types of portfolios and the many different kinds of items that can be collected. As you can see, portfolio-based assessment involves much more than collecting drawings or writing samples! It makes sense to implement portfolios one step at a time. In the following chapter, we guide you through the ten-step portfolio process so that you can enhance the reflection, communication and learning that continuously occurs in your program.

References

Bredekamp, S., and Copple, C., eds. (1997). *Developmentally Appropriate Practice in Early Childhood Programs*. Rev. ed. Washington, D.C.: National Association for the Education of Young Children.

Blome, C., and Shores, E. F. (1995). Beginning to use portfolios in the primary grades. *FOCUS* (Jan.):7-9.

Hirsch, E.S. (1984). *The Block Book*. Washington, D.C.: National Association for the Education of Young Children.

Mississippi Department of Education. (1992). *Developmental Instruction Strategies: Kindergarten Through Third Grade*. Mississippi Department of Education.

Nielsen, B. S. (1995). *Assessment Resource Handbook*. Columbia, SC: South Carolina Department of Education.

Paley, V. G. (1991). *The Boy Who Would Be a Helicopter*. Cambridge, MA: Harvard University Press. Cited in Wiltz, N. W., and Fein, G. G. (1996). Evolution of a narrative curriculum: The contributions of Vivian Gussin Paley. *Young Children* 51(3):61-68.

Taylor, J. (1996). How I learned to look at a first-grader's writing progress instead of his deficiencies. *Young Children* 51(2):38-42.

The Portfolio Book

To Learn More

Anselmo, S. (1987). *Early Childhood Development: Prenatal Through Age Eight.* Columbus, OH: Merrill.

Baroody, A. J. (1987). *Children's Mathematical Thinking: A Developmental Framework for Preschool, Primary, and Special Education Teachers.* New York: Teachers College Press.

Bartz, D., Anderson-Robinson, S., and Hillman, L. (1994). Performance assessment: Make them show what they know. *Principal* (Jan.):11-14.

Boehm, A. E., and Weinberg, R. A. (1987). *The Classroom Observer: Developing Observation Skills in Early Childhood Settings.* 2d ed. New York: Teachers College Press.

Eddowes, E. A. (1995). Drawing in early childhood: Predictable stages. *Dimensions of Early Childhood* 24(1):16-18.

Engel, B. S. (1996). Learning to look: Appreciating child art. *Young Children* 51(3):74-79.

Falk, B. (1994). *The Bronx New School: Weaving Assessment into the Fabric of Teaching and Learning.* New York: National Center for Restructuring Education, Schools, and Teaching. (Box 110, Teachers College, Columbia University, New York, NY, 10027.)

Farr, R., and Tone, B. (1994). *Portfolio and Performance Assessment: Helping Students Evaluate Their Progress as Readers and Writers.* New York: Harcourt Brace. (This book is packed with ideas for reading and writing experiences and follow-up performance assessments. It also contains a valuable discussion of the use of rubrics for evaluating entire portfolios. Recommended.)

Hyson, M. C. (1994). *The Emotional Development of Young Children: Building an Emotion-centered Curriculum.* New York: Teachers College Press.

Katz, L. G., and Chard, S. C. (1989). *Engaging Children's Minds: The Project Approach.* Norwood, NJ: Ablex.

Kellogg, R. (1970). *Analyzing Children's Art.* Palo Alto, CA: Mayfield. Linder, T. W. (1990). *Transdisciplinary Play-based Assessment: A Functional Approach to Working with Young Children.* Baltimore, MD: Paul H. Brookes Pub. Co.

Marzano, R. J., Pickering, D., and McTighe, J. (1993). *Assessing Student Outcomes: Performance Assessment Using the Dimensions of Learning Model.* Alexandria, VA: Association for Supervision and Curriculum Development.

Northeast Foundation for Children. (1987). *A Notebook for Teachers: Making Changes in the Elementary Curriculum.* Greenfield, MA: Northeast Foundation for Children.

Papalia, D. F., and Olds, S. W. (1979). *A Child's World: Infancy Through Adolescence.* 2d ed. New York: McGraw-Hill.

Perkins, H. V. (1979). *Human Development and Learning.* 2d ed. Belmong, CA: Wadsworth Pub. Co.

Peterson, R., and Felton-Collins, V. (1986). *The Piaget Handbook for Teachers and Parents: Children in the Age of Discovery, Preschool–Third Grade.* New York: Teachers College Press.

Puckett, M. B., and Black, J. K. (1994). *Authentic Assessment of the Young Child: Celebrating Development and Learning.* New York: Merrill.

Rinaldi, C. (1993). The emergent curriculum and social constructivism. In Edwards, C., Gandini, L., and Forman, G., eds., *The Hundred Languages of Children: The Reggio Emilia Approach to Early Childhood Education.* Norwood, NJ: Ablex, 101-111.

Seefeldt, C. (1995). Art: A serious work. *Young Children* 50(3):39-45

Tiedt, I. M. (1993). Collaborating to improve teacher education: A dean of education's perspective. In Guy, M. J., ed., *Teachers and Teacher Education: Essays on the National Education Goals* (Teacher Education Monograph: No. 16). Washington, D.C.: ERIC Clearinghouse on Teacher Education, American Association of Colleges for Teacher Education, 35-60.

Wiltz, N. W., and Fein, G. G. (1996). Evolution of a narrative curriculum: The contributions of Vivian Gussin Paley. *Young Children* 51(3):61-68.

Chapter 5

The Ten-Step Portfolio Process

In this chapter, we will lead you through the ten steps of our portfolio process. After establishment of a guiding portfolio policy, the steps continue with the most common portfolio strategy, collection of work samples. They culminate with using portfolios in program-to-program transitions. If you have already taken some of these steps, you will want to choose additional strategies to supplement your existing assessment system. We encourage you to take these steps in the order that works for you, because the best portfolio systems grow out of an individual learning community's interests and needs. However, most early childhood programs will benefit from beginning with the first three steps and implementing them during the first year.

The Ten-Step Portfolio Process

1. Establish a Portfolio Policy

2. Collect Work Samples

3. Take Photographs

4. Use Learning Logs

5. Interview Children

6. Take Systematic Records

7. Take Anecdotal Records

8. Prepare Narrative Reports

9. Conduct Three-way Portfolio Conferences

10. Prepare Pass-along Portfolios

For most steps in the portfolio process, we provide information in sections called *Preparation, To Begin…, Take a Bigger Step* and *Engage Families. Preparation* con-

The Portfolio Book

tains background information about the step. *To Begin…* is a set of procedures for implementing the strategy. The final two sections offer ideas for extending the strategy and for working with parents.

If you are working with a colleague or parent, talk about each step before implementing it. Work out a plan that will work for you, keeping in mind your circumstances. Set a timetable for beginning and completing the step and record your target deadlines.

Step 1
Establish a Portfolio Policy

Preparation

How do I incorporate portfolio assessment into my school or program?

What do I do with all of the material in the portfolios?

How do I score children's work samples?

How do portfolios fit with standardized tests and with report cards?

These are complex and fundamental questions about portfolio-based assessment. Each question has more than one possible answer. Designed to foster ongoing learning by children, teachers and parents, the ten-step Portfolio Process assumes the following:

1. Most material ultimately goes home with the child.

2. The portfolio is one component of an assessment system that may also include grades and limited standardized testing (this is more likely in the primary grades than in preschool), yet portfolios are the *basis* of the entire assessment system.

3. Most work samples are not scored according to rubrics (grades or scores).

But each early childhood program must answer these and other questions independently. We believe that it is critical to your success that you answer the above questions before beginning to use portfolios—and that you involve parents in developing the policy and frequently remind parents of the portfolio policy after it is adopted.

A portfolio policy is *a brief set of guidelines for collecting items for saving.* It links what is collected to your overall research and educational goals. An effective portfolio policy can influence gradual changes in curriculum and instruction. Setting a portfolio policy must begin with examining your program's or school's mission or goals. Then add your own classroom or professional goals to that list. The portfolio policy also expresses how portfolio-based assessment complements standardized assessment and reporting methods, such as standardized tests, performance-based assessment and letter grade report cards. (These are more common in the primary grades.) Here are some hypothetical examples of how the policy making process might begin:

- Your preschool is highly child-centered but uses limited methods for reporting children's progress. You may want to develop a policy of collecting evidence of developmental milestones.

- You teach in a preschool where parents value early academic skills and expect inappropriate seat work. Your portfolio policy may emphasize photography and systematic observation as ways of documenting the learning benefits of play and center time.

- A school district has in place a detailed set of curriculum objectives and an elaborate system of standardized tests for checking mastery of discrete skills and concepts. The system requires classroom teachers to administer frequent short standardized tests and record individual children's scores in an expanding database of skill mastery. In this school district, a portfolio policy emphasizing collection of *successive drafts* in different writing genres, such as essays, how-to articles and research reports, will encourage classroom teachers to strike a balance between skill drills and children's reflections.

- You teach in a school district that annually measures mastery of specific basic skills by standardized testing, and rates individual schools according to average test scores. You may want to concentrate on documenting the progress of individual children who perform poorly on the standardized tests.

- If you teach in a school with a conventional textbook-and-worksheet orientation, a policy of collecting items that reflect application of knowledge and skills to authentic activities might be in order.

A developmentally appropriate portfolio policy for early childhood programs will base collection of some items on curricular goals while encouraging children, teachers and parents to collaborate in choosing other items. It is valuable for teachers to follow specific criteria for collecting certain items for portfolios. Standardization of some selections enables future teachers to quickly follow the developmental progression in items such as drawings and work samples. The portfolio policy should ensure that you will collect such baseline samples. However, we cannot take full advantage of the power of portfolios for child-centered learning if we do not also involve the children themselves in selecting items for their portfolios. By choosing items to save and by examining those items after time has passed, children will begin to understand their own development as learners. With this understanding, they can truly collaborate with their teachers in evaluating their progress and planning their next steps.

The Portfolio Book

A clear portfolio policy should:

- Identify the purpose(s) of the portfolio, such as improving communication within the learning community

- Identify types of items to be collected

- Specify that teacher, child and parent (if possible) collaborate to select items for the permanent portfolio

- Identify the timetable, if any, for collecting each type of item

- Refer to outcomes, standards or criteria by which specific items, such as performance tasks, may be evaluated

- Stipulate that three-way portfolio conferences will be conducted at certain times of the year and at times convenient to parents

- Identify procedures for protecting confidential information

- Identify procedures for releasing items to parents and for retaining items from year to year.

Here is a sample portfolio policy that can be expanded and revised for different programs:

Each teacher at Everyday Learning Center will collect a variety of work samples, photographs, learning logs and systematic and anecdotal records in individual learning portfolios. Children and teachers will use these items during ongoing planning and assessment and as one form of documentation of individual children's progress toward the curriculum objectives of Everyday Learning Center. Teachers will summarize the evaluations they make on the basis of the portfolios in narrative reports at the conclusion of each term.

Teachers will make the learning portfolios available for children to review and will involve children in selecting items for preservation in portfolios.

Teachers will make the learning portfolios available for parents and guardians to review during regular teacher-parent-student conferences and at other times as parents or guardians request. Teachers will encourage parents and guardians to contribute items to their children's portfolios and attach their own comments about the pieces.

Teachers, children and parents or guardians will collaborate in selecting key items for preservation in pass-along portfolios. Copies of narrative reports also will be preserved in the pass-along portfolios. The remaining portfolio items will be given to the child and parents or guardians at the conclusion of the academic year.

Here is a variation of the portfolio policy for primary programs:

Each primary teacher at Creekside Elementary will collect a variety of work samples, photographs, learning logs, and systematic and anecdotal records in individual learning portfolios. Children and teachers will use these items during ongoing planning and assessment and as one form of documentation of individual children's progress toward the curriculum objectives of Shady Valley School District. Teachers will summarize the evaluations they make on the basis of the portfolios in narrative reports to accompany report cards at the conclusion of each term.

To Begin Establishing a Portfolio Policy

1. Schedule discussion(s) of portfolio policy by small groups of teachers, administrators and parents. Record comments in each small group.

2. Appoint a committee of teachers, administrators and parents to review all of the comments on portfolio policy and develop a draft policy.

3. Disseminate the draft policy and invite another round of comments.

4. Make further revisions if necessary.

5. Adopt the policy. Date the policy to prevent confusion later.

6. Disseminate the policy to all members of the community, including teachers, parents, administrators and school board members (if there are any).

7. Schedule a trial implementation period.

8. Set a time to review the policy and the process to date.

Engage Families!

Parents need to understand your overall system for assessing and evaluating their children. It is important for them to know and support the program's learning standards or criteria. Effective portfolios can help you demonstrate to parents how their children are progressing toward specific criteria, as well as capturing evidence of their children's unique qualities.

Enclose a friendly notice about the role of portfolios in your program's assessment system with each report card that goes home. Include the text of the portfolio policy in the notice. Explain parents' opportunities for reviewing portfolios. Here is an example of the kind of introductory letter you might send to parents:

Dear Families,

We are interested in how each of your children are growing and learning. We use a variety of methods to observe and document their progress. Keeping portfolios, collections of their work, as well as photographs and written records that we make, is part of our system. Your children will have many opportunities to talk about their progress and learning goals throughout the year. We want you to be involved, too. The following information explains our portfolio system and some of our efforts to make sure every family is able to participate in the life of our program. Please contact us whenever you have suggestions or questions. We want to hear from you!

Emphasize that you are interested in the parents' observations about their children's progress. Invite them to send notes, snapshots, drawings, etc., from home for inclusion in their children's portfolios.

Step 2
Collect Work Samples

Preparation

Your portfolio policy is a general guideline for the type of work samples, such as drawings, tallies of birds at a bird feeder, pictures of constructions or writing samples, that you will collect. Now you must make some additional decisions:

- Will you collect writing samples, pictures of math activities, drawings and other types of samples or some of each?

- Will you collect a specific number of samples for each child?

- Will you collect samples at regular intervals? (Weekly? Biweekly?) Or will you collect samples when it seems appropriate?

- Will you collect "best pieces," typical pieces or both?

- Will you assign a score or grade to any pieces? If so, who will create the scoring system?

We believe it is more appropriate in early childhood education to concentrate on collecting *work samples that children produce voluntarily* (authentic work samples), instead of on a fixed schedule. This helps guarantee that the samples collected will reveal the children's individual strengths. Thus some children's portfolios will eventually contain more writing samples while others contain more drawings or photographs of three-dimensional works. Please do *not* ask a child to "draw a picture with ground and sky" in order to assess the child's mastery of the schematic stage of drawing. This would be a performance task, and while performance assessments can be useful, they are a different strategy from collecting authentic work samples.

You may want children to store notes, drafts, works-in-progress and resource materials in their portfolios. We recommend that you collect work samples for a learning portfolio (see description of different types of portfolios on pages 39-41). That way, the child can save and reexamine evidence of her efforts. You may think a piece should be saved temporarily in the learning portfolio, either as a reference or model for a further learning activity or because you may want to deposit it in the pass-along portfolio later. (Remember: It is inappropriate to photocopy journal entries for collection as work samples unless the child has given permission.) If so, ask the child if she agrees to saving the piece in the learning portfolio. If she prefers to take the piece home, make a photocopy for the learning portfolio. Then, as the child completes a task or project, you can involve her in looking at, evaluating and reviewing her piece, using the method that follows. During this reflection, you discuss which of the materials are important to continue saving in the learning portfolio; perhaps some sketches would be useful in another project. Other materials may be taken home or thrown away.

The Portfolio Book

Since reproducing artwork and other multicolored pieces by color photocopying typically costs one or two dollars per copy, try to find a parent with access to a color copier who can donate this service, or negotiate a "bulk rate" with a convenient copy shop. If a parent or business donates or subsidizes color copies, always acknowledge their support in presentations, newsletters, etc.

It is best to save multiple items in each category, dating each and attaching your own observations about their significance.

Reminder: Think about what you want to assess and whether this portfolio step matches your assessment goals. Scan the other steps in the process. Would one of those strategies work better for your purposes?

To Begin Collecting Work Samples

1. Working with an individual child and following established criteria, select an item for inclusion in the learning portfolio or pass-along portfolio. Place your files or boxes and several date stamps where the children can reach them. Ask the child to sign and date the work sample and place it in his portfolio. Say, "We can look at your drawing (or story) again later and think about why it is so good."

2. Ask the child to dictate or write brief comments about the item. Use questions to help the child think about the piece. Your questions should be simple and open-ended. Stop questioning if the child seems uncomfortable with this step.

   • How did you create this piece?

   • What do you like about the piece?

   • What do you wish you had done differently?

   • Would you like to try another project like this one?

During this stage, it is important to record why the child selected a particular item. Encourage the child to dictate her thoughts: "I think this picture is very good because the fence beside the house goes straight out instead of up." You can add a comment: "Kamisha is recognizing angles and perspective in her drawings."

At first children may give one word answers or the always popular, "I don't know" response. As you work with the child using the process, over time answers become more detailed and the practice less awkward.

Talking about work samples will help prepare the children for the next steps in the portfolio process: commenting on photographs, making entries in their learning logs and participating in lengthier interviews. (A form for children's comments about work samples is shown on the next page and a reproducible page of these forms can be found in the appendix on page 144. You may want to duplicate that form, create your own or use blank paper instead of a form.)

3. Note your own brief comments, answering these questions:

- How did this task originate (teacher-initiated, child-initiated)?

- Is this a breakthrough accomplishment for this child?

- Does this sample represent progress toward a particular outcome or objective? (Make a note of the specific objective.)

- Does this sample indicate that the child is applying or extending the concept or skill in a new situation?

Making these written notations about the sample increases the value of the portfolio item and also strengthens your skills at written records. You may be able to prepare your comments at the time that you or the child select the item, or you may save that task for later. (A form for teacher comments on work samples is shown below and in a reproducible format in the appendix on page 145. Again, you may want to use our form, create your own or work without a form.)

4. Attach your comments and the child's comments to the piece if possible. For artwork, fold a small piece of paper over the top of the piece and the comments before clipping them together with a paper clip. This protects the work sample from damage. Deposit the item in the portfolio.

5. Think about how the child can reinforce or extend this learning experience. Some possibilities:

   - Replicate the piece in another medium.

   - Use the same medium for another purpose.

   - Prepare or revise the piece for publication in a class or school newsletter.

   - Demonstrate the findings to a small group or to the class.

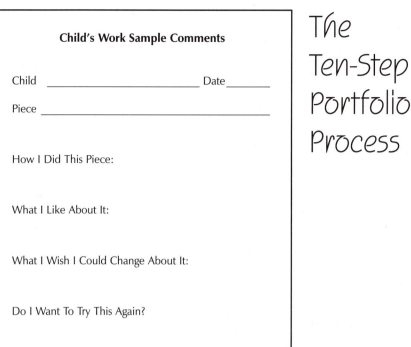

Child's Work Sample Comments

Child _____ Date_____

Piece _____

How I Did This Piece:

What I Like About It:

What I Wish I Could Change About It:

Do I Want To Try This Again?

The Ten-Step Portfolio Process

Teacher's Work Sample Comments

Child _____ Date _____

Piece _____

☐ Teacher-initiated   ☐ Child-initiated

Skill/Concept: _____

Reference: _____

☐ Beginning   ☐ Developing

☐ Mastery   ☐ Extended

Notes:

The Portfolio Book

Discuss these ideas with the child and note any decisions in your notebook or planner (see page 31-33).

6. Think about how you might use the sample to extend family involvement. Some possibilities:

   • Share the piece with parents during the next formal conference.

   • Display the piece in a classroom or hallway exhibit.

   • Publish the piece (if the child agrees) in a classroom or school newsletter, along with the child's comments about the item.

   • Encourage parents to provide the same activity at home.

   • Invite parents to participate in a follow-up activity at school.

7. Note your plan, if any, in your notebook or planner for further action.

Take a Bigger Step

Self-evaluation by children. Once the children are familiar with the procedures for commenting upon one type of work sample in the learning portfolio, you can begin to turn this responsibility over to them. Then you can add another type of work sample to the portfolios. For example, you might move from collecting drawings, to writing samples, to photographs taken by children. We encourage you to collect as many kinds of work samples as possible, because this encourages a wide variety of authentic activities in the early childhood classroom and preserves rich evidence of how exciting your classroom is!

Peer evaluation. You can enhance the collection of work samples even more by involving children in commenting on each other's work. This works best as a natural part of small group interactions, such as when children are working together on an extended project. For example, preschoolers at work on a block "town" probably will talk about their construction site. You can ask children in this type of play situation if you may record some of their comments on chart paper (but do not let your assessment of their activity overwhelm their play). In a primary program, a child may have written a draft monologue for a skit. You can suggest, "Ask Janelle to be your audience and practice giving your speech. Find out if she thinks it's ready."

You also can establish formal procedures in certain situations for evaluation and revision within small groups. Share with the group, in a checklist or rating scale that is clear and easy to use, the learning objectives that you have established for their work. Ask the group to evaluate its own work according to this instrument. Use their conclusions to plan, *with the children,* follow-up activities to address any weaknesses. (We do not encourage class-wide peer evaluation rituals because these are not likely to encourage meaningful reflection and communication by children.)

Saving work in the pass-along portfolio. Occasionally, you will want to suggest to a child that a finished piece be transferred to the pass-along portfolio (see description of a pass-along portfolio on pages 40-41). Most children will eventually want to select finished pieces for the pass-along portfolio themselves. We will consider the child's role in creating the pass-along portfolio more in Step Ten—Using Portfolios in Transitions.

Engage Families!

Bulletin board displays, newsletters and PTA meetings are good opportunities for sharing work samples with the wider learning community:

- Involve children in creating a bulletin board display for an open house, or use an easel display to place the display near an entrance for parents to see at drop-off and pick-up times. Use their own dictated or written comments as text panels for the display. Change these displays often.

- With children's permission, reproduce a few drawings in the school newsletter and write a brief explanation of how children develop as artists.

- Produce a five-minute slide show with a title such as "The Recent Works of Six Year Old Artists" for the next parent meeting. Take the work samples to a photography shop to have copy slides made. The cost for copy slides will be about $2.00 per work sample; call around for the best price. In narrating the show, give a little background on the learning outcomes that the samples reflect. If a slide show would be too costly, tape samples to the wall and point to the drawings as you talk about each one.

- To support parents who may not have transportation, encourage parents to carpool to meetings when possible. (A neighborhood mapping project would be a good time to let parents know about children and families who live nearby—and encourage carpooling!)

- Child care may be an issue for some parents. School programs and PTA meetings should be planned to include child care for parents who request it in advance.

Encourage families to reflect on their own work. Design "family-work" activities (instead of homework!). At the end of the activity include a step that helps families reflect on the experience by posing a few questions, such as:

- Was this activity interesting? Enjoyable?

- List two things you each learned from this activity.

- Can you repeat this activity again at home, perhaps in a different form?

Step 3
Take Photographs

Preparation

This step is to *take frequent photographs of children and their activities*. We recommend that you invest in one of the good "point-and-shoot" cameras that are available. (See appendix page 152-153.) This is a relatively expensive step in the portfolio process that some programs may have to postpone, but we recommend it as Step Three because it helps you prepare for keeping written records. However, implementation of the rest of the ten-step process is certainly possible without photography.

If your program cannot purchase a camera and film, investigate grant possibilities, contributions by local businesses and assistance by high school or college photography labs. Some parents may be able to donate a camera or film. If necessary, schedule time for fundraising as you prepare for this step. Recruit parents to help! (Two or three teachers or caregivers may be able to share a camera, but the logistical problems in this arrangement can be significant enough to undermine the technique, so we do not recommend it except where educators work as a team in a single classroom or family day care home.)

Once you have your camera, keep it loaded and handy but out of reach of the children. (If possible, keep a second, less expensive camera on hand for children to use!) Try to shoot a few pictures each week whenever important events occur. Avoid asking children to pose for photographs, for this will alter the course of events even as you are photographing them. In the beginning, children will notice that you are taking pictures and will want to "smile for the camera." Encourage them to pretend you are not there. They will soon become accustomed to the camera and ignore you.

It is very important to make notes of the scenes as you photograph them. You can use a small spiral notebook for this purpose, storing it with the camera between shoots. Save the notes until you have the prints and then transfer them to individual children's portfolios. (When their programs can financially support it, some teachers find it handy to dictate their observations about the photograph into a small hand-held tape recorder and transcribe them each day or two.)

Reminder: Think about what you want to assess and whether this portfolio step matches your assessment goals. Scan the other steps in the process. Would one of those strategies work better for your purposes?

To Begin Taking Photographs

1. Take enough time to compose your shot. You don't need to worry about the artistic quality of your photographs, but you do want to be sure they tell the

story. Get children's faces so that you can identify them later. Get a little of the background so that you will be able to note where the event occurred. If you are photographing a construction project, take close-ups so that children's hands are visible; if your point is to capture a moment in the social life of the class, step back for a candid group shot. Watch the flash signal and don't snap the next shot until you know the flash is ready.

2. Record brief notes of the incident or object you have photographed. Include the date, setting, names of the children involved and the significance of each scene.

3. Have each roll of film processed as soon as you are through with it. Order double prints; with duplicates you will have pictures for more than one child's portfolio and will occasionally have a spare to give to a parent.

4. When the prints arrive, immediately note the dates and pertinent details on the envelope ("Cindy Smith's kindergarten, Week of March 25") and store the negatives, in the envelope, in a sturdy box.

5. Review the notes you made about the incidents or objects when you photographed them. Decide whether the comments are sufficient or whether you should make additional notes. Ask yourself:

- What was happening when I took this photograph?

- What happened just before? Just after?

- Who was present?

- Did I plan this activity, did a child or was it spontaneous?

- What kind of learning was happening here—cognitive, social-emotional or physical development?

- Was this a milestone for any child?

The questions above will help you think about what is important to record.

Work sample courtesy of the Educational Research Center at Florida State University.

6. Attach your comments to the backs of the prints. Use good-quality adhesive notes; they will adhere better to the coated surface of photographs. This method is preferable to writing on the backs of prints, because both pens and pencils can damage photographs.

7. If you want to attach photographs to existing anecdotal records, lengthier written records, work samples or other items already in the portfolios, fold small rectangles of paper over the photographs before using paper clips to attach the photographs to the work samples, written records or anecdotal records.

8. Think about how you can use the photographs to involve families.

The Portfolio Book

Take a Bigger Step

Once you are familiar with handling a camera and preserving photographs in children's portfolios, you can extend this strategy by involving children in the process. Looking at photographs engages children in thinking about their own accomplishments—and in the process of selecting items for inclusion in portfolios. Most children enjoy looking at pictures of themselves. They closely examine each picture to find themselves. They like to talk about what was happening when the photographs were taken. You can take advantage of this typical enjoyment of photographs as a first stage in involving them in assembling their own portfolios.

You might announce during a whole-group period that you have received a new batch of pictures from the developer. Mention that you could use some help in remembering what was happening in the pictures and then make the prints available at a table for children to examine during choice time. (It will be wise to have separated duplicates and negatives and put them safely away.) Provide pencils and adhesive notes so that children can dictate or write their own recollections of the events. It will be fine for more than one child to attach a note to a photograph. If the notes are significant evidence of multiple children's writing progress or other development, you can photocopy the prints, attach the children's notes and insert them in their portfolios.

In small groups or one-on-one situations, you can talk with children about their recollections of the photographs, your own thoughts about their significance and the possibility of inserting them in their portfolios.

Whether you use photographs or another type of evidence, such as artwork, writing samples or a videotape, as the springboard for children's participation in portfolio collection, make your initial conversations with the children casual. To say, "Now we will talk about these photographs" will probably puzzle or intimidate the children. Ideally, joint decisions about adding items to portfolios occur naturally. In time, remarks like, "That would be a good picture to put in your portfolio" will inspire the children to make suggestions such as, "Let's put this in my portfolio" and (even more exciting) "David should take a picture of that for his portfolio. It's the best castle moat he ever dug."

Once you have engaged the children's interest in portfolio collection through photographs (or another strategy), you can involve them more systematically in the process of portfolio-based assessment. Announce the arrival of a new set of prints during a whole group time. Make the prints available at the writing center along with forms for children's comments. Invite them to write or dictate comments about any of the photos that interest them. Add the children's comments and the photographs to their portfolios. (If two or more children select the same photograph, make black-and-white photocopies of the print or order duplicate color prints.)

Next, promote any children who are interested to classroom photographers! Story reenactments, block constructions, dances and other gross motor activities are good subjects for children's photographs. Provide an inexpensive back-up camera for the children to use. Follow the same photo procedure, involving the children as much as possible. This provides the opportunity for children to function as journalists in the classroom, taking photographs and making notes about what is happening. They will become more aware of their own progress at the same time that they practice important skills in authentic activities. (If you involve children in taking photographs for portfolio purposes, you will need to help them learn to handle the camera and understand that not every situation needs to be documented in this way.)

You can also extend photography by using the photographs in newsletters, articles, slide presentations, videotapes and other formats. *Important*: Before using photographs of children in a brochure about your program, a slide presentation or a publication, it is important to obtain parental permission. (A sample photo release form can be found on appendix page 146.)

Videophotography is another extension of this strategy. Special educators use audio and video recordings successfully for assessment and evaluation, but these techniques are less common in general education settings. Children enjoy evaluating videotapes of their own and each other's demonstrations. You can purchase a videotape for each child and add to it over time. Introduce the narration of each new segment with the date and a brief explanation such as "April 17: Kevin's Description of His Building Project." (Early childhood programs with sophisticated computers can even store segments of video in individual electronic portfolios, although this is an optional and extremely expensive storage method.)

Engage Families!

To use photography as a springboard for greater family participation, you can share your photographs with parents.

- Take the negatives to a photography shop to have copy slides made. The cost for copy slides will be about $2.00 per negative; call around for the best price. Use the photographs in a brief slide show for a parent meeting or open house. Involve children in narrating the show! Many families have cameras but rarely use them except to record formal occasions such as birthday parties and holidays. Encourage the families with cameras to take pictures often, to teach their children to use their cameras and to work with their children to prepare written captions for family photo albums.

- Invite parents to send snapshots of family activities to school for inclusion in their children's portfolios. Think about ways that the children can extend their family experiences at school. Perhaps a vacation trip to visit cousins could be the topic of a travel essay, or an outing to a ball game could inspire a research project. A set of photographs can become the illustrations for an original, handmade book about a family reunion; invite all of the members of the family to write portions of the text, or appoint the child's grandfather editor of the project.

Videotapes of classroom activities are another form of documentation that can give families a new window on their children's daily lives. Deborah Greenwood, in an article in the journal *Young Children*, recommended recording videos of special events in the center or school and allowing children to take them home on a rotating schedule. For parents who do not own television sets or videocassette players, be sure to provide a video corner at open houses or show the tapes during conferences with parents.

Step 4
Conduct Learning Log Conferences

Preparation

Collection of work samples and photography have begun to enable you and your children to reflect on what has been learned. The next step is to *meet regularly with individual children to talk over the variety of their recent activities*. You and the child can record their thoughts and plans in a special notebook that we call a learning log.

As we explained on pages 54-57, the learning log is an ongoing record, written by the child and the teacher, of new discoveries and understandings. It is different from a typical journal because it is the product of regular, one-on-one conferences between child and teacher or caregiver. The learning log allows you to preserve evidence of individual children's understanding and thought processes. This evidence can then point you to follow-up activities that will reinforce and extend the new knowledge and even enable children to teach each other. Additionally, learning logs also are a device for structuring and focusing one-on-one conferences with children, an important technique in portfolio-based assessment.

We suggest that you incorporate learning logs into the classroom routine gradually, so that children are familiar with the purpose of the documentation, before you begin formal one-on-one learning log conferences.

Duplicate the learning log form on appendix page 147 (or create your own) and put several copies in a three-prong folder for each child. Label the folders with their names and store the logs in children's learning portfolios. Be sure that they are handy for impromptu conferences. As children become acquainted with the process, you can ease out of using the forms and have children keep their learning logs in blank notebooks of various kinds.

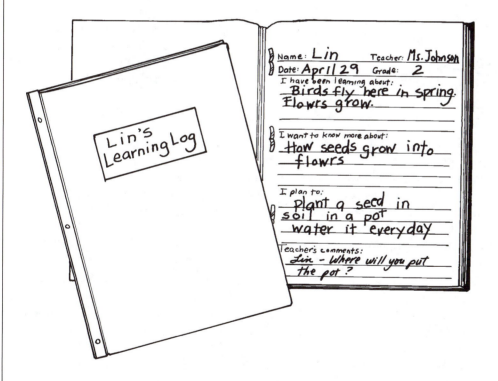

Write your own learning log entry and copy it on a poster or butcher paper for posting on a wall where children can see it. As soon as possible, copy an early learning log entry by one of the children (with the child's permission!) for another example.

Name: Ms. Johnson   Grade 2
Date: March 4
I have been learning about:

_____

_____

_____

I want to learn more about:

_____

_____

I plan to:

_____

_____

_____

Encourage the children to talk about what they have experienced at home as well as at their school or child care program. As topics arise, demonstrate how to write in the learning log during sessions with individual children, small groups or the whole group, according to their interests. Discussions of both familiar and new learning topics will encourage children to constantly explore, ask questions and test theories. As children review what they know about a topic and ask additional questions, the learning log becomes documentation of their unfolding understanding. You also can use the learning log conference to review a child's drawing or draft of writing or performance assessment or work on a test. If you teach in a primary program and are still recording letter grades (and we suggest that you do so as long as parents desire grades), the learning log conference is an appropriate time to discuss grades with children, offering praise or reassurance as necessary.

Ideas for learning log topics may develop at any time. Keep a small notebook in your pocket for recording observations during small-group and whole-group times, so that you can write down ideas for learning log conference topics as they come to you. Suggest the ideas to individual children as soon as possible and encourage them to write or dictate their thoughts on a learning log form.

Once the class is familiar with the concept of learning logs, decide how often you will conduct formal one-on-one learning log conferences. Weekly conferences are probably appropriate for most preschool and primary-grade children. If you schedule four or five brief learning log conferences per day, you should be able to meet with all children in the course of a week. In a program that has been based on whole-group activities, the shift will need to be planned carefully and implemented gradually. Center time, when children work in small groups on a variety of activities, may be the best period for conducting learning log conferences. A classroom aide or volunteer may be helpful as you begin to devote more time to one-on-one sessions with children.

Learning Log Time

1. *Prepare learning logs for all children and keep them nearby during whole-group discussions.*

2. *Conduct "Learning Log Time" each day and invite children to share stories of experiences at school and at home. Ask questions like, "What did you do yesterday that was interesting or fun?" Look for the learning that occurs in all kinds of children's experiences, from reading a new book to visiting a park to seeing a new baby cousin. Write short summaries of different children's experiences, along with ideas for extending the learning, on chart paper: "Blake learned that the new park downtown has a fun place for skating. Let's write to the Parks Department for a map of the new park." "Natasha learned that new babies sleep a whole lot. Let's look for library books about what new babies do." Allow these whole-group sessions to continue for as long as children have learning experiences to report.*

3. *Wrap up these whole-group discussions with a quick report of something you learned since the last discussion and how you will learn more. Model writing your learning log entry on chart paper and talk about how you decide what to write. Encourage the children to make their own suggestions for what you should write. Continue modeling your own learning log for one to two weeks, always inviting the children's participation in the process.*

4. *Once the whole-group Learning Log Time is a comfortable routine for the children, encourage them to begin keeping their own learning logs (dictating or writing in the logs). Start with the children who are the most skilled writers or the most verbal participants in Learning Log Time. Demonstrate how they can write or dictate their entries in their personal logs during whole-group sessions.*

5. *Eventually, divide children into learning log groups for weekly sessions. Place skilled writers and "loggers" with emerging "loggers" and work with several children at once, so that they can observe each other's progress.*

6. *Incorporate group learning log conferences into your center time schedule so that each child participates in a weekly small-group learning log conference at a conference table. The schedule might look like this:*

The Portfolio Book

Reminder: Think about what you want to assess and whether this portfolio step matches your assessment goals. Scan the other steps in the process. Would one of those strategies work better for your purposes?

Learning Log Conference Schedule

Monday Group

James

Natasha

Brittney

Joshua

Tuesday Group

Elmer

Charles

Jett

Akins

Wednesday Group

Angela

Lisa

Nick

Scott

Thursday Group

Bradley

Gary

Marquez

Pima

Maria

Friday Group

Robin

Stephen

Frederick

Danisha

Five-year-old Jessica reports during a whole group period that when she visited her grandparents over the weekend, she helped make ice cream and cake. After she tells her story, her teacher, Mrs. Chandler, says, "Jessica, I'm glad you told us about making ice cream and cake. If you will bring me your learning log after Together Time, I'll help you write that down."

Together Jessica and Mrs. Chandler write about making ice cream and cake. The teacher points out the cooking utensils and measuring cups at the science center and suggests that they plan a time to make cupcakes at school. She makes a note in her planner to invite Jessica's grandparents to help with the project.

Mrs. Chandler notes that Jessica dictated instructions for making ice cream and cake. She also notes the learning objectives that Jessica's experience and the learning log conference meet:

- *Participate in speaking activities.*

- *Write for a variety of purposes.*

- *Understand that texts have different purposes.*

- *Describe ways food is produced/processed/distributed.*

Put into Learning Log format, the information from the above whole-group time would look like the following on a Learning Log form:

Learning Log

Name __Jessica Lewis__   Teacher __Mrs. Chandler__

Date __March 12__   Grade __2__

I have been learning about:

how to make ice cream and cake. You mix
milk and eggs and sugar and crank it for a long
time. You freeze the ice cream. You cook
the cake in the oven. You put flour in the cake.

I want to learn more about:

How to make a cake with decorations on it.

I plan to:

Make cupcakes with frosting in different colors.

Teacher's Notes: Dictated instructions.
Ask grandmother to volunteer w/cupcakes?
Objectives LA-02RI-011, LA-02RI-027, LA-02RI-044, SC-02RI-019

Source: Little Rock (AR) School District Curriculum Objectives, 1996.

The Portfolio Book

To Begin Using Learning Logs

1. During the learning log conference, ask the child about what she has learned at school or at home in the past week. What was interesting, fun, challenging? If the child has previously mentioned an interesting learning experience, remind her now.

2. Record her comments or assist her to write her own entry.

3. Ask her to think about what she would like to do to learn more about the topic at hand. (This step will require prompting with many children in the beginning. If you suggest ideas for new learning activities, be sure to write down the goals that the child supports.)

4. Help the child think through specific actions that will help her meet those goals. Write these steps down so that section of the log form is an action plan for the child.

5. In the section for teacher's notes, note any outcomes, objectives or criteria that the child's activities meet.

6. Record anything that needs follow-up: ways to involve families, siblings, children in other classes, community resources.

Take a Bigger Step

Regularly review the learning logs, checking for opportunities to integrate children's interests and experiences into small-group or whole-group activities. For example, perhaps two or three children report that they went to a car show with family members. You can pull them together in a small group for a short-term project about new cars. Or perhaps you have planned to read aloud a book by Frances Hoban and you learn that Lynette has read a different Hoban book at home; you can ask her to share that book with the class before or after your read-aloud session.

Engage Families!

When children report experiences at home, on weekends and on vacations, during learning log conferences or at other times, let their parents know that you are interested in their home learning activities. Take a few moments to jot a quick note to the parents. (Print the note so those children beginning to read might be able to read it to their parents.) Ask the child to put it in her backpack and take it home to mom or dad.

The learning log can become a family learning log. Encourage children to take their logs home and share them with family members. Urge parents to make their own entries, such as descriptions of their children's activities or special family projects. Nadine Harding introduced "family journals" as a format for written three-way communication and invited parents to record their notes of their children's home reading activities (Harding, 1996). Some parents grabbed the opportunity to become penpals with their children's teacher, but not all did. She reflected later in an article in the journal *Young Children* that "what I have learned is that I have to continue to find ways to reach each and every family."

Step 5
Conduct Interviews

Preparation

The interview is an extension of the learning log conference. It is *a technique for probing more deeply into what a child knows and can do in a specific area*. You learn more about how the individual child learns, what she knows best and, consequently, how to teach her more effectively in the future.

After you have established a routine for learning log conferences, and children are comfortable in brief one-on-one discussions about what they are learning, you can begin to occasionally conduct longer interviews. Rather than simply responding to the child's cues, you can plan to inquire about a particular topic.

To prepare for this step, think about skills or concepts that you would like to assess through interviews. Perhaps there are skills that do not lend themselves to traditional tests. Children may be able to demonstrate deeper understanding of a particular concept through discussion than by writing or demonstrations. You may have realized that collecting work samples and photography are not effective techniques for assessing children's mastery of a particular content area. Select a single area for assessment and plan to interview the children over several weeks, allowing ample time for testing and refining this assessment technique.

Interviewing is a technique that requires practice. The questions that you ask now may be very simple compared to the questions you ask three years from now. In time, your teaching goals, and perhaps even action research, will guide you in asking deeper and deeper questions. Meanwhile, take your time. Even if your early attempts at interviews do not yield all of the assessment information you would like, you are giving the child a rare chance for meaningful, one-on-one attention.

After experimenting with interviewing, you may want to incorporate this assessment technique into a particular unit of study more systematically. Think about how best to apply this technique in your curriculum.

Tips for successful interviews. Fortunately, most children enjoy talking about themselves and their work, even if they feel they are not doing well. These tips can help you take advantage of young children's natural inclination to talk about what they are learning:

The Portfolio Book

- Plan an interview to assess an individual child's mastery of a specific skill, concept or topic, such as retelling a familiar story with a new ending. Make a list of questions to use as a guide during the interview. Examples:

    1) Did he look at the picture book before dictating his new version?

    2) Did he draw illustrations before or after dictating his story?

    3) Does he have additional ideas for his story?

- "Ice-breakers" are important in interviews. Begin the interview with something that is sure to interest the child, and let him talk! Make notes of these comments, even if they are not your true objective, so the child will become comfortable with the interview process. You might mention seeing the child at a local park and ask whether he enjoys going to the park.

- Rephrase a question if the child does not understand it, to be sure that the child truly does not know the answer. "Where did you get the idea for your new ending?" may be clearer than "Was a book in the reading center your source for this new ending?"

- Make it clear to the child that you are very interested in what he has to say. Sit at his level and look in his eyes. Nod your head. Make comments like "That's interesting" or "I'm impressed that you know that."

- Use a combination of short-answer and open-ended questions. If a child falters at an open-ended question, try another short-answer question. Do not make the child feel that he is inadequate in the interview situation. For example, if the child looks puzzled when you ask, "How did you start making up your story?", ask, "Did you think of the flying dragons before you thought of the boy?"

- If the child wanders from the subject, gently guide him back once you are sure he is not leading up to a relevant statement. Do not interrupt or reprimand the child for changing the subject. Example: "I'm very interested in how you thought of your story about flying dragons. Can you tell me more about that?"

- Take accurate, legible notes of your questions and the child's responses.

- Fast note-taking is important. A good interview can grind to a halt if you have to repeatedly say, "Please wait while I write that down!" If you are not quick with a pencil, use a tape recorder. As your note-taking skills improve, you probably will use the tape recorder less often.

- It is important not to misquote a child. Always ask the child to clarify statements that are not clear. Tell him, "I want to be sure that I understand you. Can you tell me that again?" If his statement is still not clear, ask him, "Do you mean . . . ?"

- Pay attention to the unexpected! The child may surprise you with statements that will be the most valuable information you obtain in the interview.

Tips for taking notes. The interview is the first strategy in the ten-step portfolio process that involves extensive note-taking. You may already have developed your own personal shorthand for taking notes. If not, now is the time to begin. An inexperienced note-taker takes lengthy notes. With practice, you will recognize what is most important to write down and take fewer notes.

- Date your notes at the beginning.

- Note the setting.

- Concentrate on writing down the child's important comments.

- Be sure to use quotation marks when you write a child's comment just as he said it.

- Draw a star or asterisk beside key points as you write them, to indicate that these ideas were important to the child.

- Record your impressions of the interview, such as "Eleanor was fidgety" or "David seemed to enjoy the chance to talk." Use parentheses to distinguish these perceptions from facts such as "David kept his mittens on." Write simple phrases and sentences. Clear writing is better than flowery writing.

If you do not make a back-up audiotape of the interview, transfer your notes to a complete, systematic record of the interview as soon as possible, before you forget the details and are unable to make sense of your notes. Write your perceptions and opinions of the interview in a separate section and label it "Comments."

Making Audiotapes. Although you may not want to tape-record every interview, this is a valuable option. Written notes, transcripts or audiotapes of interviews can go in children's portfolios. You can transcribe interviews of groups and deposit a copy of the transcript in each participating child's portfolio. (See appendix page 153 for information about tape recorders.)

Before recording an interview, take a few minutes to experiment with the recorder so that you are comfortable operating it. When you are ready to begin recording interviews, label a tape for each child with his full name. Store the recorder and tapes in easy reach, but above children's grasp if they are not old enough to handle tapes carefully.

Immediately after making a recording, note the date and a one- or two-word cue to the nature of the recording on the cardboard liner in the tape case. Return tapes to their cases and the storage bins without rewinding, so that you can add each recording to the earlier material. You may want to write a supplemental comment about the taped episode to add to the child's private portfolio.

In transcribing tape-recorded interviews, it is not necessary to include every "um" and "ahh" that your subject uses. Skip over those in order to produce a clear, readable transcript. On the other hand, it will probably be appropriate to preserve mistakes in grammar or word choice that the child makes, in order to have an accurate record of the child's verbal skills at the time of the interview.

The Portfolio Book

Reminder: Think about what you want to assess and whether this portfolio step matches your assessment goals. Scan the other steps in the process. Would one of those strategies work better for your purposes?

Mrs. Alexander wants to assess Nicholas's competence to plan and conduct a simple investigation, one of her school district's required learning objectives for first-graders. She has observed Nicholas at the science center for several days but has not seen clear evidence that Nicholas can pose scientific questions and search for answers. She decides to try an interview.

Mrs. Alexander asks Nicholas to meet her at the science center during center time. She says, "I'm wondering if you have tried looking things up at the science center. Do you have any ideas about how we could find the name of this shell?"

Nicholas answers that they can look in the book about shells for pictures that resemble the shell. When they find that several pictures seem to resemble their shell, Mrs. Alexander asks him what he can do next. Nicholas points out that some of the pictured shells are from the Pacific Ocean and only one is from the Gulf Coast. A label on the classroom shell indicates that it came from Texas, and by consulting a map, Nicholas is able to determine that the shell must be from the Gulf Coast.

Mrs. Alexander congratulates Nicholas on his successful investigation and then makes a systematic record of his performance. During a review period later on, Mrs. Alexander locates the science and geography objectives that correspond to Nicholas's work and adds a notation to the systematic record.

Example of a tape case record with several recordings logged, including a spontaneous recording as well as an interview.

90 minutes

IEC I / TYPE I

B DATE/TIME
   NOISE REDUCTION

A DATE/TIME
   NOISE REDUCTION

Nicholas Benton

9.17.96
Reading journal entry

10.22.96
Reading a book

11.27.96
Talking at Math Ctr.

2.5.97
Interview: Science Ctr.

To Begin Interviewing Children

1. Decide to interview one or more children on a particular topic.

2. Plan a time and setting for the interview that will allow you and the child to be undisturbed, if possible. Schedule more time than you think you will need. Your experience with learning log conferences should guide you here; children will vary in their ability to participate in interviews. (Some children may not be appropriate subjects for interviews at all. One important benefit of portfolio-based assessment is that it provides a variety of assessment strategies to meet the needs of different children, so it is not critical to interview every child.)

3. Tell the child in advance that you want to talk with him about the topic. Say something like, "I want to know what you think about it." Tell the child you would like him to bring any materials that relate to the topic with him.

4. Review the child's learning portfolio for information and "ice-breakers" that will be helpful.

5. Shortly before the scheduled time, remind the child to gather his learning portfolio or other materials for the interview.

6. Explain that you want to record his comments in writing or on the tape recorder. Demonstrate how you are noting the date, his name and your name.

7. Conduct the interview.

8. Conclude the interview by helping the child add notes to her learning log or by modeling how to write her own reflections on the matter at hand.

9. Review your notes. Think about whether the interview yielded the information you needed. Think about whether your ice-breaker conversation yielded information that is useful. (Perhaps young Jose told you that he mastered a new stunt on his in-line skates. Could that be a topic for a writing project?)

10. Transcribe the interview if you used a tape recorder. Summarize the interview in a systematic record. Note achievement of any outcomes or objectives, or any areas that need additional work, in the comments section of the systematic record. Place the transcript and the systematic record in the child's portfolio.

11. Return the audiotape to the tape storage container.

I really had fun when I learned how to

The Ten-Step Portfolio Process

The Portfolio Book

Take a Bigger Step

Once the process of conducting tape-recorded one-on-one interviews is in place, you can extend it by recording class discussions. By listening to these discussions later, you may find evidence of children's understandings or misconceptions that you did not immediately notice.

A tape-recorded interview can be a valuable "wrap-up" procedure for concluding a child-initiated project. If several children participated in the project, you can record a small-group interview. Notes or a transcript of the interview might serve as a starting point for an oral or written report or demonstration by the group. The children may feel more comfortable with making a presentation to the class after answering your questions about their project in an interview situation.

Try recording other events in the classroom: children singing, reading aloud or discussing a science experiment. Use individual children's tapes and record the date and type of incident before recording the children. Log these events on the tape box in the same way that you log formal interviews.

Reminder: After mastering this technique in your classroom, think about whether regular learning log conferences and periodic interviews are both necessary for all of the children. Can one technique or the other suffice for any particular children? Can you combine features of the two techniques when assessing some children? Make these techniques work for you and for the children by combining, collapsing or extending them as necessary for individual children.

Engage Families!

Parents love to hear audiotapes of their children, so use the tapes to encourage greater family involvement.

Play recent segments of children's tapes during conferences with their parents. Encourage children to explain to parents what was occurring when the recording was made.

Present tapes to parents when their children leave your classroom or program.

Encourage families that have tape recorders to make audio recordings of family events:

- Conversation around the kitchen table when cousins come to visit

- Children's performances of favorite songs, poems, stories and even bits of movie dialogue.

Audiotapes are also a good means of communication with parents who have limited vision or literacy skills. Record a friendly, informal explanation of work samples or other materials that you are sending home and place the tape, materials and a portable tape player in a backpack. (Try giving the child a lesson in operating the tape player so that he can share his new skill with family members.)

Step 6
Make Systematic Records

Preparation

In the ten-step portfolio process, systematic records are *notes that you plan to make of particular children's actions in specific situations*. They flow nicely from learning logs because you can observe and record the activities that you and the child plan during the learning log conference. Systematic observation of children's activities also can help you evaluate the effectiveness of particular instructional strategies and individual children's specific skills or concepts. For example, if you set a goal of enhancing the science learning in your classroom and plan to provide a variety of concrete experiences at the science center, you may want to take systematic records of children's responses to those opportunities. If you find through observation that few children are using the science center's new prism properly, you will know that you need to demonstrate how to use the prism to different small groups.

Now that you have prepared written comments and made written records of children's comments in interviews, you are ready for the next writing task of making systematic records. This step has the extra benefit of preparing you to make anecdotal records, when you will recognize and record important evidence as you observe it.

As written records, notes of systematic observations are more challenging than your brief comments on work samples, photographs and learning logs, or even your notes of interviews. You may want to review the general comments about written records in Chapter Four (pages 58-65).

Posing a question. It is important to pose a clear question that can be answered through systematic observation. Be as specific as possible. Using this note-taking strategy to find out "how Billy is doing in math" might be difficult or frustrating. Do you want to find out whether Billy can locate math materials? Or is your question really whether Billy pays attention to demonstrations of math activities? Perhaps you want to observe whether Billy turns to other children at the math center for help or advice, or always struggles through a problem on his own. The tighter the focus of your observations, the better your chances of actually recording the information that you need.

Avoiding bias. Another challenge of keeping systematic and anecdotal records is to avoid bias. The difference between *descriptive language* and *evaluative language* is important here. You must describe only what you really see, not what you expect to see or would like to see. It also is important to separate your factual account of events from any comments that you make about the episode. You can practice this by working with a portfolio partner. Plan for both of you to make notes of a particular situation or event. Compare your notes and discuss any conflicts in your observations. This exercise will help you refine your skill at objective note-taking. Continue to practice until you and your partner usually make highly similar observations, always preserving confidentiality.

The Portfolio Book

Of course, simply choosing certain actions to observe and record is a biased activity, because you are creating a written record that emphasizes certain aspects of a child's behavior and ignores other aspects. This is why portfolio-based assessment is valuable. Using different assessment strategies insures that more aspects of a child's growth and development will be assessed and evaluated.

Practice first! To help the children become comfortable with your new note-taking behavior, conduct practice systematic observations. Explain that you will be writing down what you see happening and that you will not be able to talk with the children while you are watching and writing. Practice this enough times for the children to get used to this new activity. This practice will help you recognize the kinds of behavior that can be assessed through systematic observation.

Privacy issues. Before using systematic observation as part of portfolio-based assessment, you may want to discuss the privacy issues with your center or school administrator. A center or school policy on when to request parental permission would be helpful. We encourage you to inform the child and the parent, whenever practical, that you plan to conduct systematic observations. For example, if you are interested in how much Sam seeks other children's ideas when he works at the math center, you might tell him, "I want to learn more about how you work at the math center, so I'm going to be watching and making some notes. When I'm through, I'll show you what I wrote down."

Once you have identified a subject and a particular behavior for systematic observation, plan when you will make your observations and how many times. We recommend that you conduct observations of the same behavior for three days in a row, to be sure that you are observing genuinely typical behavior.

After conducting systematic observations, it is critical that you evaluate whether this strategy yielded the information that you needed. If you cannot draw clear conclusions from the evidence gathered through systematic observation, you can use additional assessment techniques, such as an interview or performance assessment, to verify your interpretation.

Note-taking for systematic records is similar to making notes of interviews (Step Five). Here are some additional tips:

- Observe the child's actions and concentrate on recording them. Do not speculate about the child's motives or feelings.

- Note the time at several points during the observation.

- Record the events in proper sequence. Use arrows to indicate the sequence if you do not write down every event as it occurs.

- Describe important details of the surrounding scene. Is the child working in a crowded area? Is the room hot or cold? Is the subject's best buddy absent? With practice, you will be able to quickly recognize the factors that may be relevant and quickly record them. For example, the absence of a seven-year-old's best friend and usual science buddy could be important. The color of his shirt probably is not!

- Summarize your notes in a formal systematic record. Make your writing thorough and precise. Don't write "Josepha was moody during center time." Instead, write "Josepha smiled and talked with friends when she entered the block area. Within 30 seconds, she hit Shaquil when Shaquil refused to give her a toy boat."

We do not recommend using a hand-held tape recorder for dictating notes of systematic observations. These tools are useful for dictating spontaneous or anecdotal observations (Step Seven) because in that technique you are essentially reacting to an event just after it occurs. However, in systematic observation, when you are attempting to observe a child's typical behavior as it occurs, without altering that behavior, dictation could be obtrusive.

Reminder: Think about what you want to assess and whether this portfolio step matches your assessment goals. Scan the other steps in the process. Would one of those strategies work better for your purposes?

Systematic Observations

March 11

James

Whole second-grade class reviewing homework: a reading reflection about a story in basal reader. J. is busy erasing and rewriting another paper, but volunteers immed. when called upon. He reads his answer to a worksheet qstn.

T. calls on different children to read paragraphs of the basal story aloud. J. appears to not pay attn., but reads immed. when called. Reads in a halting monotone, not pausing for punctuation. Less expressive than about half of readers. Gets stuck on "proclamation," "issued," "whoever."

J. turns page of bk. with others. On second rdg., only gets stuck on "hugged." Not pausing for punctuation.

T. poses questions about story. J. raises hand eagerly to answer ea. qstn. Called, he gives lengthy, thoughtful answer, filling in with "uh" several times. Turns and fidgets as t. asks for ideas for imaginary want ad. Called upon: "I'd just use the book." "I'd do what he did" (indicating another child).

The Portfolio Book

March 12

James

Whole class follows tcher's directions to build circuits and illuminate light bulbs. J. participates in small group. Does not volunteer to answer qstns.

March 13

James

T. calls on children to review yesterday's circuit activity. J. raises hand, answers. Clear, knowledgeable.

T. calls on different children to read aloud from short book about electricity and light. J. reads in halting monotone, not pausing for punctuation. Stuck on "bouncing," "off." On second reading, still not expressive. Stuck on "either," "bounces," and "off."

Comments

James's mother asked for information about his fluency at reading aloud. During three daily systematic observations, I observed that James understood a work of fiction and scientific information and was able to discuss the materials during question-and-answer sessions. His speech during conversation is punctuated by many "uhs" and he reads aloud with some difficulty. It is my impression that James' verbal ability does not fully reveal his thorough mastery of concepts and information.

To Begin Making Systematic Records

1. After deciding to conduct systematic observations of a particular child, obtain the parent's permission if necessary.

2. Schedule the observations and add them to your notebook or planner.

3. Arrange for a colleague or assistant to handle your usual tasks while you make the observations.

4. Inform the child that you will be making notes at a particular time.

5. Conduct the observations and make notes of the child's actions. Concentrate on descriptions, not evaluations.

6. After each observation, ask yourself, "Have I described all of the circumstances that relate to this incident?" Add details that you can remember. If you realize that you have overlooked important details, schedule another observation to replace the incomplete one.

7. Summarize your systematic observations in a systematic record form (sample shown below and on a reproducible page on appendix page148). Include the date and your reasons for conducting the observations. Refer the reader to any other items in the portfolio that relate to the subject of the record.

8. Share your observations with the child during a learning log or portfolio conference, if appropriate. Encourage him to comment on your observations through writing or dictation. Date his comments and attach them to the systematic record.

9. Plan additional assessments, such as interviews or collecting work samples, to supplement your systematic observations.

Take a Bigger Step

After systematic record-keeping has become an easy habit in the classroom, you may want to expand your records by adding separate comments, reflections or follow-up plans to your systematic observations.

Systematic observations can become a rich part of the early childhood curriculum. Once you are a frequent note-taker, you may want to involve the children in the process. Preschoolers may suggest that you make notes of interesting events. Primary-grade children can even make their own notes of classroom activities, events on the playground or in the cafeteria or wildlife behavior.

Systemic Record

Child _____ Date _____

Recorder _____ Time ____ to _____

Permission for Observation Granted by_____

Activity or Behavior:

Setting:

Details:

Reason for Observation:

Comments:

Engage Families!

For ethical reasons, it is important to determine whether you are invading a child's privacy by conducting systematic observations. A simple way to handle this issue is by asking the child and the child's parent for permission to observe the child. This may seem like an unnecessary or time-consuming step, but it has two important benefits. First, it involves the parents in your ongoing assessment and evaluation of their child. Second, it protects you from challenges later on.

When you decide that it would be useful to observe a child's actions in a particular situation, write the parents a clear, straightforward note about your plans. Invite their input as you prepare to assess their child through systematic observation. You also can encourage them to implement this assessment strategy at home, if possible. Here is an example of a note to parents:

Dear Mr. and Mrs. Jones:

I have noticed that Michael rarely completes classroom assignments on schedule. I would like to observe him during work periods to discover what difficulties he is having. Please indicate below if you have any objections to this plan and return this slip to me by Monday.

Your observations of Michael's activities at home would be helpful. Does he complete tasks at home (such as putting away his clothes or writing a thank-you note) in a timely manner, or does he seem to have trouble completing them?

Please call me or drop me a note if you have thoughts about why Michael is having a little trouble with classwork right now.

Thank you!

Step 7
Make Anecdotal Records

Preparation

Anecdotal record-keeping involves *recognizing important developmental events in individual children's lives as they occur and writing brief, clear accounts of those events.* The caregiver or teacher functions like the "beat reporter": ever alert to news as it happens, constantly checking all of her important sources and observing all of the activities on her beat—the classroom or family child care home. Making useful anecdotal records requires a working knowledge of child development and the goals and objectives for your program. It also requires that you be able to think and write on your feet!

Once you have thoroughly mastered Steps One through Six in the ten-step portfolio process, Step Seven, anecdotal record-keeping, will be simple. You will have already learned the skills that you need. By applying various portfolio strategies to all of the domains of children's growth and development, you have learned how to look at the whole child. By conducting regular learning log conferences with individual children, you have developed a deeper knowledge of each child's interests, needs and abilities than you ever had before. By writing captions for work samples and photographs, comments on learning log entries, summaries of interviews and systematic records, you have sharpened your writing skills and overcome any apprehension that you may have had of writing. You will have acquired all of the equipment you need. You will even have developed your own personal shorthand method.

Now all you have to do is put on your beat reporter's hat. Carry your notepad and a good pen with you all of the time. As you observe and participate in classroom activities, make quick notes of everything that seems important. Regularly review the skills and concepts that you are currently incorporating into learning activities, as a refresher course of what to watch for.

As an alternative, you can dictate quick notes into a small cassette recorder. Tape recorders are especially suited to anecdotal record-keeping because the unplanned nature of the technique means that you are not striving to stay in the background of activities. You can carry the recorder with you throughout the day and transfer your dictated notes to anecdotal record forms at the end of the day.

A few more tips about taking anecdotal records:

- *Limit your account to one incident.*

- *Complete your notes as soon as possible.*

- *Just the facts!*

- *Record any comments about the incident in a separate section of your anecdotal record form.*

- *Refer to supporting information, such as work samples or photographs, in the comment section.*

We do not recommend that you plan to make a standard number of anecdotal records for each child in your class. This could turn the most powerful portfolio strategy into a crushing load of busywork. Instead, concentrate on observing individual children in various situations and making notes of significant events. If you find over time that your anecdotal records tend to be about only a few children or situations, then you can plan to pay more attention to other children and situations. (Those observations would produce systematic records because you planned them.) The number of anecdotal records you make probably will vary with changes in your curriculum and classroom schedule, from a low of just one or two a day to perhaps five a day. If you find this technique as rewarding as we expect, you probably will make more and more such records as time goes by.

The Portfolio Book

To Begin Making Anecdotal Records

1. Write your observations as events occur, so that your records are accurate.

2. Note the child's name, the date and the details of the incident.

3. Capture the action in phrases, not complete sentences, and use abbreviations wherever possible. Concentrate on description.

4. As part of wrap-up and planning for the next day, review any notes you have made each day and decide which records are worth preserving. Transfer those notes to anecdotal record forms and add comments, if any. (A sample anecdotal record form can be found on appendix page 149.)

5. Share your observations with the child during a learning log or portfolio conference, if appropriate. Encourage him to comment on your observations through writing or dictation. Date his comments and attach them to the anecdotal record.

Anecdotal Record

Child *Anika L.* Date *2/18/97*

Event: A. sucked her thumb, put her head on the table, + refused to participate

Setting: Whole-group reading

Details: A. was asked to read aloud two different times, Declined both times & began sucking her thumb 2nd time.

Comments: 1st time I've observed A. sucking thumb. Need to assess reading

Recorder: *EJS*

one-on-one —

example of completed anecdotal record form

example of hand-written quick note

Tues -
Reading Time

Anika sucked her thumb and put her head down when asked to discuss rdg. selection.

EJ

Take a Bigger Step

Anecdotal records are priceless "local color" for explanations of your classroom practice. Write a letter to parents or an article for the center's newsletter. Start with an anecdotal record (changing the child's name if appropriate) and then explain the significance of the event to your goals and the child's development.

Engage Families!

Parents appreciate news about their children's activities at school or the child care program. You do not have to save all of the information you gather through anecdotal record-keeping for formal conferences with parents. Anecdotal records are a rich source of material for occasional quick notes to individual parents about wonderful things their children did.

As you review the day's anecdotal notes and decide which events to preserve on anecdotal record forms, you can take a few extra moments to jot a note to a parent about one of the episodes you recorded. You can use any sort of small notepad or reproduce the Anecdotal Note Form shown below and found in reproducible form on appendix page 150.

News Flash Form ▶

For parents who you know have limited literacy skills, or who have not responded to past written messages, try telephone calls.

You might set a goal of communicating one anecdotal record to a parent each day. We do not recommend a checklist or schedule for these notes, but you should try to spread the good news around and be sure that, over time, all parents receive notes or calls from you.

Communicating good news about children's activities is an important prelude to formal conferences with parents, when you may have to address concerns about their children's development. Sharing good news first will demonstrate that you have positive regard for their children.

Child _____ Date_____

News Flash!

I observed the following incident today and thought you would want to know:

_____

Teacher

Observation is an important part of our assessment system. We learn more about how children are growing and learning by observing them often. I will share more news about your child's progress with you at our next conference, but please call me any time you have questions.

Remember that I'm always interested in news from home about your child's activities! Please encourage your child to share news of special experiences at school during class discussions or in his or her journal.

Step 8
Prepare Narrative Reports

Preparation

If you have followed the ten-step portfolio process and are comfortable with each of the earlier steps, you now have the information and skills, and you are ready to prepare narrative reports! Nonetheless, you may be thinking, "I already collect work samples, conduct learning log conferences and interviews and make sys-

The Portfolio Book

tematic and anecdotal records. Narrative reports seem to be just more paperwork, a rehash of what I have already done. Good grief!" Good points. You have done a great deal of work already. Narrative reports are, in fact, *summaries of your findings about an individual child's growth and development during a specified reporting period.* But we think there are at least four good reasons for taking this step in the process.

Four Reasons to Write Narrative Reports

- *Parents will appreciate your summary of their children's development. Many of them probably will keep your narrative reports about their wonderful, unique child's development for decades.*

- *Step Eight helps prepare you for Step Nine, the three-way portfolio conference with parent and child.*

- *Writing narrative reports involves you in systematically reviewing the contents of the portfolio and correlating children's activities to extrinsic standards or criteria.*

- *Narrative reports simplify the overall assessment system. As you prepare for a child's transition to another class or program, you can turn over most of the portfolio contents to the child and family. Your narrative reports will be the core of the pass-along portfolio—briefing papers, if you will, for the child's next teacher. A few key work samples will provide illustrations for the summary statements you make in the narrative reports. Thus, Step Eight also prepares you for Step Ten—Using Portfolios in Transitions.*

The contents of portfolios, along with confidential material and notes about individual children in your *teaching journal,* if you keep one, are the sources for your narrative reports.

Narrative reports do not have to be lengthy (four to eight paragraphs is sufficient) but they should be thorough. An outline such as the following will help you cover the important topics. (Notice that we include social-emotional development, but only as one of three developmental domains. A common mistake is to devote entire narrative reports to children's behavior. Remember: parents are also interested in their children's academic progress.)

Outline for Narrative Reports

- *Summary of Child's Progress Since Last Report (or since the last parent-teacher conference, or during the current school year)*

- *Key Developments*

   Communication
   Mathematics

Problem-solving
Creativity
Social-emotional
Physical
Literacy
- *Action Plan*

With practice, preparing narrative reports will take less time. A word processor will make this step easier, although it is not essential. In the beginning, however, we recommend that you stagger preparation and dissemination of these reports. For example, if you issue reports or report cards in November, February and May, you can send home narrative reports for a fourth of your children each week during those months. Assuming a group of 20 children, your schedule of narrative reports would look like this:

Schedule of Narrative Reports

November

Week One	*5 reports*
Week Two	*5 reports*
Week Three	*5 reports*
Week Four	*5 reports*

February

Week One	*5 reports*
Week Two	*5 reports*
Week Three	*5 reports*
Week Four	*5 reports*

May

Week One	*5 reports*
Week Two	*5 reports*
Week Three	*5 reports*
Week Four	*5 reports*

To Begin Preparing Narrative Reports

1. Schedule time for writing narrative reports. If possible, arrange for an aide or parent volunteer to take over your class to allow you some extra time.

2. Review a child's portfolio, making notes for each section of the report. Some items will yield information for just one section; others will relate to several sections.

3. Draft a thesis statement or main point for each section. Number your comments about various portfolio items that you want to use as back-up for your thesis statement.

4. Ask yourself, "Is any pattern or trend apparent?" Draft these observations, if any, for the summary.

5. Write the sections. Polish.

6. Ask yourself, "Have I overlooked any important areas? Do I need to plan systematic observations or other portfolio techniques to assess this child's development in those areas?" Note any plans for future assessment in the action plan section.

7. Preserve one copy of the narrative report in the child's private portfolio and send another copy to the parent.

Narrative Report

March 17

Toni, age 4 years

This is a report of Toni's progress in different curriculum areas since January 10. Sources of evidence are noted in parentheses. Toni is progressing in all areas and is noticeably enthusiastic about working with blocks, puzzles and water.

Key Developments

Communication

Toni continues to participate in ordinary classroom conversations with other children. She uses sentences that include two or more ideas with descriptive details. On Feb. 9, she said to me, "Ms. Terry, I am going to take the baby and put the yellow dress with blue flowers on it. Then I am going to make spaghetti with meatballs and red sauce for us to eat tonight." (Feb. 9 anecdotal record)

Since the last report, Toni has begun to use expressive language instead of hitting when she becomes angry with another child. Several times during the past two months, Toni has told a child or a few children that she didn't like the way they took her puzzle or book, rather than hit them. We are working to reinforce this behavior and to encourage it so she will use words rather than fists when angry. She has also begun to ask the teacher to help her in solving problems with others when her conversations don't get the results she wants. (Jan. 30, Feb. 9, Feb. 10, March 10 systematic records)

Toni continues to follow directions given by the teachers without any difficulty, demonstrating receptive language. (March 10 systematic record)

Mathematics

Toni continues to group objects together that are the same in some ways but different in other ways (blue chips and blue bears). She is beginning to use words such as "some," "not," and "all" in the proper way, but often gets confused when using the words "some" and "all." Toni is still working to place four or more graduated items in order (tallest to shortest) and is making progress in using comparison words correctly in conversation. ("He is bigger than I.") Toni has now mastered correctly counting up to 6 objects. (Jan. 20 learning log conference; March 9, 10 systematic records; March 11 interview)

Problem Solving

Toni makes daily choices on where she wants to go during center time. When she is in the centers, she usually chooses activities that involve working with her hands. She prefers art, puzzles, blocks and water centers. Toni is showing persistence in problem-solving since the last reporting period. Toni tries at home as well as school to figure out how to work puzzles and does not give up or get angry when the first try does not succeed. (Centers choice chart; three-way portfolio conference)

Creativity

During this reporting period, Toni demonstrated her ability to use blocks to make a house with a chimney, steps and door. She has painted several pictures that show she is beginning to include details such as hair bows, earrings and bracelets in her self-portrait. (Work samples)

Social-Emotional

We have been working with Toni on more appropriate social interactions with other children. She is calling some classmates her friends and does not take toys or learning games from children as often as we observed four months ago. She is making progress in sharing and taking turns. We will continue to work with Toni on how to interact with children in ways that build friendships. (Jan. 30, Feb. 9, Feb. 10, March 10 systematic records)

Physical

Toni continues to show progress in other areas such as running and walking. She is now consistently catching bean bags using both hands. She responds to the steady beat of songs by clapping her hands to the beat. Since the last reporting period, Toni has become more skilled in using markers and pencils. This is noted in the greater detail in her pictures. (Feb. 12 anecdotal record; work samples)

Literacy

Toni continues to picture-read, telling the story from the pictures in the book. She begins on the left side of the page when reading the story. She usually answers questions about a story that has been read. She can identify the letters in her first name and since the last reporting period can identify 4 of the 6 letters in her last name. (Feb. 3 learning log conference)

Action Plan

We will continue to provide a variety of learning opportunities for Toni, including her favorite "hands-on" activities and more opportunities to strengthen social skills such as verbal communication and sharing. We will also insure that our program provides enough toys and books for all children so that sharing is not a constant expectation.

Take a Bigger Step

You can extend the benefits of this systematic review of portfolios by involving other teachers or related professionals. Request time during a staff meeting or in-service roundtable to present a child's portfolio, explaining your observations and conclusions and how the portfolio items support them.

You can also use this process during team decisions about referring individual children to special services.

Step 9
Conduct Three-way Portfolio Conferences

Preparation

Enabling children to think about their own development as learners, and to set goals for themselves, is a critical part of portfolio-based assessment. Therefore, involving children themselves in the use of portfolios is the crucial turning point in the implementation process, the step that makes the portfolio more than a mere work folder. This is the step that transforms your classroom from a *hierarchical system*, in which the teacher makes all decisions, to a *community of learners*—where everyone is thinking, planning, reviewing and revising their work.

Of course, the portfolios will hardly have been a secret from the children until now. Ideally, they have joined you in selecting, labeling and saving work samples. They have observed you making anecdotal records and photographing classroom events. They know that you store these items and frequently refer to them. They have participated in learning log conferences and interviews, so one-on-one reflection will be comfortable for them. Now it is time to involve the children, and eventually their parents, in looking at their entire portfolios and evaluating their progress over a longer period. No matter how proficient you become at using portfolios, this is a step that you will repeat each year as you introduce the portfolio process to a new group of children and families.

We make this a separate step, and almost the last one, to emphasize that—just as you cannot transform how you assess and evaluate children overnight—children cannot immediately develop the skills and habits of mind to seriously reflect on their own learning. This step should not be rushed. (We have observed highly frustrated children who were, with considerable fanfare, escorted to a "portfolio party," complete with punch and cookies, at which they were supposed to review their portfolios with their parents. The portfolios were identical sets of performance tasks that did not actually reflect the children's individual interests. Many of the parents did not attend, being unfamiliar with the concept of portfolios. But the biggest problem was that the children did not know what was expected of them.)

Once children are familiar with examining their own work and talking about it, you can challenge them to think about how they could improve their work. Self-evaluation depends upon clear criteria or standards. While the criteria may be external (such as objectives for math learning), we believe that children become lifelong learners when they are able to establish their own criteria. For example, a child might observe that he has written about soccer almost exclusively over the last several months. He might decide to draw upon all of his soccer knowledge to write a comprehensive article on the game, or he might decide that it is time to use his sports-writing skills on baseball. These are different, but equally valid, writing goals. Once he writes down or dictates his new goal, dates it and adds it to his learning log, he has a clear criterion by which to judge his future work. During the next portfolio conference, it would be a simple matter to pose the question, "Have you met your writing goal yet?"

Step Nine is not possible in a classroom where children are not already accustomed to handling important responsibilities. If you are not yet comfortable with allowing the children the responsibility of moving about the classroom, exchanging ideas and gathering and replacing materials, then you may want to first examine ways of changing your classroom practices to support child-directed learning.

Two-way portfolio conferences. Serious reflection is not a quick business. In fact, as children become more thoughtful and skilled at evaluating their own work, they will need more time, not less, for portfolio conferences. We recommend that you work toward conducting individual two-way portfolio conferences several times

The Portfolio Book

each year and eventually on a monthly basis. You may want to adapt your daily schedule to permit a single portfolio conference per day. While the formal portfolio conference will not be the only time that you spend with individual children, scheduling the conferences will guarantee that you get to every child regularly. You can hold these portfolio conferences during established learning log conference periods in the classroom. It is not necessary to emphasize to the children that you are implementing a new assessment strategy. A low-key statement like, "Let's get out your whole portfolio and look at it today" is more appropriate. Use the same techniques as in learning log conferences and interviews, but direct the child's attention to her body of work. (You also should continue to meet with children for weekly or biweekly learning log conferences.)

You can begin the portfolio conference by examining new and old items with the child. Ask some focusing questions:

- What kinds of pieces are in your portfolio?

- Which pieces do you think are your best?

- Which would you like to have done differently?

- Which pieces show your progress as a writer? As a mathematician? A scientist? An artist? A researcher?

You might observe that his recent stories are much longer than one written in November. Ask, "What are you doing now to make your stories longer?" If you are examining photographs of block constructions, you can ask, "What is different about these?" in order to assess the child's understanding of his own progress. If you need to check his mastery of certain math skills, you might ask, "Can you remember what we learned about addition when we played with blocks?" Give him time to answer thoughtfully and write down his responses. Explain that you are interested in his ideas and want to remember them. Write down the child's comments, take dictation or ask her to write her own reflections about her portfolios in her learning log.

Topic lists can be useful for children who have trouble planning new writing projects. During portfolio conferences, you can ask children for topics for future pieces. Help them record those ideas on a "Topic List" to be saved in their portfolio. When a young writer is temporarily blocked (it happens to all of us!), you can help by referring the child to her topic list. For example, if a child often writes about new clothes, you could suggest that she write about clothes she wore as a baby, clothes that girls wore when her parents were children or the differences between clothes for school, for chores and for dress-up occasions.

Journals are another good source of writing topics. A writer who is searching for a new idea might find several in past journal entries. With some suggestions for expanding the piece from the teacher, a three-sentence entry about a weekend trip could become the basis for a playdough sculpture or a page-long story.

Next, help the child set goals for his work. At future portfolio conferences, he can think about whether he has met the goals and, if not, revise his work in order to do so.

At the conclusion of each portfolio conference, collaborate with the child to write a summary of his progress, goals and objectives in a learning log entry. The emerging writer can dictate the summary, perhaps after some modeling by the teacher. More experienced writers can prepare the summaries themselves, creating authentic records of how they think about their own work.

After the conference, you may want to preserve your impressions or concerns in a written record of your own. Be clear and objective! Any document you create can reflect upon the child in the future. Date your written record and refer to it in planning mini-lessons for the child and others.

Be patient! With your encouragement, children will gradually assume more and more responsibility for participating in these discussions. The portfolio conference may inspire some children to revisit an earlier project, perhaps adding new touches to a piece of artwork or revising a book review. A portfolio conference allows you to discover more about what the child thinks of his own work and progress. At the same time, you may be able to model how a child can evaluate his own work.

Many teachers like to engage their children in decorating portfolios with self-portraits or writing introductory essays about themselves. These tasks may give children a sense of "ownership" of their portfolios, but they are class-wide teacher-directed activities that do little to support individual children's learning. On the other hand, if a particular child paints a self-portrait, it would be valuable to make a full-color photocopy of the work to add to the portfolio. Our point here is that devoting time to decorating portfolios or furnishing them with look-alike writing assignments contradicts the underlying purpose of portfolio-based assessment, which is to enable children to reflect upon their progress and set their own learning goals.

Peer evaluation. Some primary teachers expect children to evaluate each other's work and even to comment on each other's portfolios. Sometimes these exercises involve children in talking informally or in pairs; other times the children write responses to each other's works. This is a refashioning of the traditional "Swap papers!" command that came after tests, saving the teacher from the chore of marking every test and allowing word to spread through the class about who received As and who received Fs.

While we think that young children can learn much from each other, and that the developmentally appropriate early childhood classroom allows a great deal of conversation and sharing, we fear that these "peer evaluations" can become rote activities with little value. Confidentiality is another important concern. Learners of every age need to know that their works-in-progress are respected and that they, and they alone, may decide when to share them. Thus, we do not recommend formal peer evaluations of the learning portfolio. (See page 92 for a description of how peers can be involved in the collection of work samples.)

Moving from two-way to three-way portfolio conferences. After the children are comfortable with discussing the items in their portfolios with you, and with writing or dictating comments on the portfolios in their learning logs, you can introduce the concept that other persons can learn about them by examining their portfolios. During the first year that you implement portfolio conferences, you may want to begin conducting them with children in the winter and then involve parents in the spring. In subsequent years, you may be able to use the steps in the portfolio process from the beginning of each year.

When you are ready to invite parents to the center or school or home for three-way portfolio conferences, we recommend that you schedule the conferences before your deadlines for preparing narrative reports, so that you can include new information that children and/or parents provide, and any plans that you, the children and the parents make together, in the reports.

If some parents do not speak English (or the primary language in your program), make arrangements for a translator. Even when you have a translator, we recommend that you learn and practice a few key sentences in the parents' language, to demonstrate your good faith and sincere desire to communicate with them. One sentence might express your gratitude for a parent's attending the conference. Another might emphasize significant aspects of the individual child's progress. A third might ask for the parent's suggestions concerning a specific issue.

If you have used the ten-step process, parents may already know that you are preparing narrative reports, so you can invite them to the portfolio conferences by saying, "I want to share with you how I review your child's work in order to prepare the (quarterly) narrative report. I also want to include your observations and ideas in the narrative report."

Many parents will want to spend considerable time examining their children's portfolios. We suggest that you allow 30 minutes for each conference. If you schedule one per day, it should take about four weeks to hold conferences with all of the children's parents and guardians. You may be able to have these conferences during a planning period or near pick-up time.

Other parents may be unable or unwilling to participate in portfolio conferences. The variety of family involvement strategies in the ten-step portfolio process will provide alternatives for those parents. Children may feel hurt or embarrassed if their parents do not participate, so avoid emphasizing their parents' noninvolvement in portfolio conferences. Sending the learning portfolio home with the child for parents to examine is a possible option, if you are confident that the family will return the material. A home visit is another option.

Of course, you certainly should make the learning portfolios available to parents whenever they visit the classroom.

To Begin Three-way Portfolio Conferences

1. Schedule each three-way portfolio conference in cooperation with parents. Allow 30 minutes per conference.

2. Advise each child of the upcoming conference. You might say, "We're going to be able to show your parents all of the work you have done recently."

3. Give the child the opportunity to add comments or explanatory material to her portfolio. This could take the form of a brief audio message or remarks that she can plan to make during the conference.

4. Conduct the conference, making notes as you do in an interview with the child. Invite parents and children to comment on individual items or the entire portfolio. You can include their verbal comments in your notes of the conference, provide a form for written comments or tape-record the parent's comments on the child's audiotape. (If you use audiotape, be sure to state the date, the parent's full name and an explanation of the setting, such as "Three-way Portfolio Conference," before taping the parent.)

5. Add plans or outcomes from the portfolio conference to the narrative report.

Take a Bigger Step

The underlying purpose of three-way conferences is not just to show young children's work to their parents. It is to elicit the parents' ideas about their children's learning. Once you have established a smooth routine for three-way conferences, challenge yourself to plan questions for different parents that relate to their children and families. Also use the conference to engage parents in classroom activities, specific projects or field trips. Use the reproducible letter on page 151 to start a deeper dialogue with parents.

Engage Families!

Margaret Puckett and Janet Black, in their book, *Authentic Assessment of the Young Child: Celebrating Development and Learning*, suggest placing portfolio conferences on your center's or school's master calendar in order to give parents plenty of notice of conference weeks. Devise a general schedule, such as conferences for children with last names beginning with A through G will be during the first week of the month. Of course, you will need to rearrange some conferences to meet parents' schedules. Arranging transportation and holding some Saturday conferences may help some parents. It is important to make sure that every child's family is able to participate in a portfolio conference.

When you are ready to hold three-way portfolio conferences, give parents a concrete experience of portfolio-based assessment. Invite them to write letters about their children for inclusion in the portfolios. Provide writing prompts to make the activity easier.

Writing Prompts for Parents

- *Tell me about your child's favorite game.*

- *Tell me about a time in the day or week when your child enjoys talking with you.*

- *Tell me about any chores that your child performs at home.*

Make the letters optional and provide a second opportunity to dictate comments for inclusion in the portfolio during each portfolio conference. A form for parents' letters can be found on appendix page 151.

Step 10
Use Portfolios in Transitions

Preparation

As we explained in Chapter Four on pages 40-41, the third type of portfolio is the permanent, pass-along portfolio that accompanies the young child from the preschool years through the primary program and beyond—while the children and families keep most of the contents of the learning portfolios. The pass-along portfolio is *a slender collection of work samples, narrative reports and other essential documents that each new teacher can use as the basis for initial decisions about the individual child.* Preparing pass-along portfolios is an important step in the ten-step portfolio process because it allows you to involve parents in creating lasting records about their children's learning.

If your program's portfolio policy does not address the transfer and use of pass-along portfolios, now is the time to amend the policy. Establish criteria for preserving items; perhaps one piece should reflect the child's writing ability and another his mathematical skill. Decide on a maximum number of work samples to add to the pass-along portfolio each year and stipulate that selection of those items should occur during the final three-way portfolio conference of the year. Be clear about how future teachers should use the portfolios: as references in initial communication with children and families, in designing individual and small-group projects, etc.

Plan procedures for storing the pass-along portfolios between sessions, delivering them to the next-year teachers and returning them to the permanent portfolio archive. We suggest that a set of file cabinets be devoted to this archive and that teachers and administrators use a check-out system to track location of the pass-along portfolios when they are in use.

It is very important that the child and family participate in selecting pieces for the pass-along portfolio. Talking with children about recent pieces of work during a portfolio conference naturally leads them to selecting pieces for inclusion in pass-along portfolios. However, young children may initially be unable to select their own "best works" or "typical works" for their portfolios. One way to introduce the practice of selecting items is to model your own portfolio process. If you have been keeping a portfolio of your own work, share it with the children. Explain that you are adding a piece because it has a certain significance.

Having your help in selecting pieces can be the demonstration they need to eventually make these decisions on their own. One approach is to ask children to select three pieces at a time, with no particular criteria. Tell them that you must agree with them about one of the pieces. During conferences to discuss their selections, you can elicit their thoughts about their work and at the same time model using different criteria—choosing a drawing, choosing a story with dialogue, choosing a math project that they completed with a buddy. (Worksheets are not valuable items in portfolios, or in early childhood programs, for that matter, because they do not reflect authentic work. Gently discourage children from choosing worksheets. Use this opportunity to examine the use of worksheets in your school or program.)

Following your program's established portfolio policy, you can select additional items as necessary for the pass-along portfolio. We recommend including a copy of each narrative report.

To Begin Preparing Pass-along Portfolios

1. Schedule the final three-way portfolio conference of the year. Send a special note to parents, advising them that you need their help in selecting items for the pass-along portfolio.

2. Before the final three-way conference, ask children to think about which items they would like for future teachers to see. Give them ample time to review their learning portfolios and make choices. Children can select their "best" or favorite works in art, writing (or dictation), mathematics and other areas. Make photocopies or photographs of these works, so that the child can keep the originals, and suggest that the child write or dictate a note to the next teacher about one or more of the pieces' significance.

3. Before each three-way conference, make your own tentative choices for the child's pass-along portfolio. Attach simple notes to the items to help you explain your thoughts to parents.

4. During the three-way conference, spread out the child's portfolio contents. Show the parent your choices and the child's choices. Ask him for his thoughts. (If a parent strongly desires that a particular item be added to the pass-along portfolio, add the item even if it does not meet the criteria for selection. Attach

a note explaining the parent's thoughts about the piece, or invite the parent to do so himself. Do not indicate to the parent that you are "going against policy" to accommodate him. Part of the purpose and value of portfolios is the involvement of parents in the ongoing assessment of their children.)

5. Make final choices, balancing the child's, parent's and your professional interests. Make photocopies, include photographs or color slides of bulky or fragile items such as block constructions or tempera paintings. Whenever possible, give original pieces to the child to take home, along with the contents of the learning portfolio.

6. Be sure that each item is clearly labeled with the child's full name, the date of the work and a brief comment about its significance.

7. Deposit the child's complete pass-along portfolio in your program's portfolio archive.

Take a Bigger Step

Help the next teacher by attaching "Special Facts" to the portfolio copy of the final narrative report on each child. You might write that a particular child greatly enjoyed using interlocking blocks at the block center, or that a child planned to read all of Beverly Cleary's books during the summer. Encourage the next teacher to acknowledge these "special facts" in postcards to his or her rising children before the next year begins. Do the same yourself!

After you and your program have established a policy and procedures for preserving portfolios from year to year, the next step is to send portfolios with children who transfer to another program or school.

References

Greenwood, D. (1995). Home-school connection via video. *Young Children* 50(6):66.

Harding, N. (1996). Family journals: The bridge from school to home and back again. *Young Children* 51(2):27-30.

Herman, J. L., Aschbaher, P. R., and Winters, L. (1992). *A Practical Guide to Alternative Assessment*. Alexandria, VA: Association for Supervision and Curriculum Development.

Puckett, M. B., and Black, J. K. (1994). *Authentic Assessment of the Young Child: Celebrating Development and Learning*. New York: Merrill.

To Learn More

Alberto, P. A., and Troutman, A. C. (1990). *Applied Behavior Analysis for Teachers*. 3d ed. Columbus, OH: Merrill. (This textbook includes clear explanations and charts for using interval recording, time sampling, duration and latency recording, and other techniques of formal systematic observation.)

Almy, M., and Genishi, C. (1979). *Ways of Studying Children: An Observation Manual for Early Childhood Teachers*. New York: Teachers College Press.

Boehm, A. E., and Weinberg, R. A. (1987). *The Classroom Observer: Developing Observation Skills in Early Childhood Settings*. 2d ed. New York: Teachers College Press.

Clemmons, J., Laase, L., Cooper, D., Areglado, N., and Dill, M. (1993). *Portfolios in the Classroom: A Teacher's Sourcebook*. New York: Scholastic Professional Books. (A brief, useful summary of five elementary school educators' techniques for incorporating portfolios. This book includes reproducible forms.)

DeVries, R., and Kohlberg, L. (1987). *Constructivist Early Education: Overview and Comparison with Other Programs*. Washington, D.C.: National Association for the Education of Young Children. Cited in Burchfield, D. W. (1996). Teaching all children: Developmentally appropriate curricular and instructional strategies in primary-grade classrooms. *Young Children* 52(1):4-10.

The Portfolio Book

Duckworth, E. (1996). *"The Having of Wonderful Ideas" and Other Essays on Teaching and Learning.* New York: Teachers College Press.

Falk, B. (1994). *The Bronx New School: Weaving Assessment into the Fabric of Teaching and Learning.* New York: National Center for Restructuring Education, Schools, and Teaching.

Farr, R., and Tone, B. (1994). *Portfolio and Performance Assessment: Helping Students Evaluate Their Progress as Readers and Writers.* New York: Harcourt Brace.

Gallas, K. (1995). *Talking their Way into Science: Hearing Children's Questions and Theories, Responding with Curricula.* New York: Teachers College Press.

Gardner, H. (1993). *Multiple Intelligences: The Theory in Practice; A Reader.* New York: Basic Books.

Gilbert J. C. (1993). *Portfolio Resource Guide: Creating and Using Portfolios in the Classroom.* Ottawa, KS: The Writing Conference.

Grosvenor, L. et al. (1993). *Student Portfolios.* Washington, D.C.: National Education Assocation.

Helton, J. (Undated). Appropriate strategies for improving math portfolios: A comparison of self-assessment versus peer conferencing. Lexington, KY: University of Kentucky Institute on Education Reform. (An eighth-grade math teacher reports on her comparison of two evaluation strategies. This is a good example of action research. UKERA #0008. Available from Institute on Education Reform, 101 Taylor Education Bldg., University of Kentucky, Lexington, KY, 40506-0001.)

Hill, B. C., and Ruptic, C. A. (1994). *Practical Aspects of Authentic Assessment: Putting the Pieces Together.* Norwood, MA: Christopher-Gordon Publishers. (This book is a thorough treatment of authentic assessment in the cognitive domain. The authors devised dozens of forms which can be duplicated or adapted.)

Linder, T. W. (1990). *Transdisciplinary Play-based Assessment: A Functional Approach to Working with Young Children.* Baltimore, MD: Paul H. Brookes Publishing Co. (This is an excellent guide to Linder's technique for observing children's developmentment across the domains and preparing formal reports. The book includes observation guidelines and checklists. Parent involvement is an important part of Linder's approach.)

National Association for the Education of Young Children. (1996). Responding to linguistic and cultural diversity: Recommendations for effective early childhood education. *Young Children* 51(2):4-12.

National Council of Teachers of Mathematics. (1989). *Curriculum and Evaluation Standards for School Mathematics.* Reston, VA: National Council of Teachers of Mathematics.

Neill, M., Bursh, P., Schaeffere, B., Thall, C., Yohe, M., and Zappardino, P. (1995). *Implementing Performance Assessments: A Guide to Classroom, School and System Reform*. Cambridge, MA: The National Center for Fair and Open Testing. (The section, "Organzing for Change: What You Can Do," is particularly helpful in the process of establishing a portfolio policy. Available from Fair Test, 342 Broadway, Cambridge, MA, 02139.)

Sachs, B. M. (1966). *The Student, the Interview, and the Curriculum*. Boston: Houghton Mifflin Co.

Tiedt, I. M. (1993). Collaborating to improve teacher education: A dean of education's perspective. In Guy, M.J., ed., (1993). *Teachers and Teacher Education: Essays on the National Education Goals* (Teacher Education Monograph: No. 16). Washington, D.C.: ERIC Clearinghouse on Teacher Education, American Association of Colleges for Teacher Education, 35-60.

Vincent, L., Davis, J., Brown, P., Broome, K., Miller, J., and Gruenewald, L. (1983). *Parent Inventory of Child Development in Non-school Environments*. Madison, WI: Madison Metropolitan School District Early Childhood Program. (Cited in Turnbull and Turnbull, 1986, 210.)

Voss, M. M. (1992). Portfolios in first grade: A teacher's discoveries. In Graves, D. H., and Sunstein, B. S., eds., *Portfolio Portraits*. Portsmouth, NH: Heinemann, 18.

Whitebook, M., and Bellm, D. (1996). Mentoring for early childhood teachers and providers: Building upon and extending tradition. *Young Children* 52(1):59-64.

Wiltz, N. W., and Fein, G. G. (1996). Evolution of a narrative curriculum: The contributions of Vivian Gussin Paley. *Young Children* 51(3):61-68.

Wolf, C. P. (1988). Opening up assessment. *Educational Leadership* 45(4):24-29. Cited in Graves, D. H., and Sunstein, B. S., eds., (1992). *Portfolio Portraits*. Portsmouth, NH: Heinemann.

Chapter 6

Conclusions

The ten-step portfolio process that we describe in this book fosters continuous reflection and communication in a community of learners, including both young children and all the adults in the children's lives! It can lead you to individualization of curriculum and instruction, continuous professional development and greater family involvement. The more thoroughly you implement these portfolio techniques, the more you will learn about child development, curricula and standards and effective classroom practices. For many teachers, using portfolios becomes part of a wider, deeper exploration of teaching and learning.

After reflecting on the process of implementing portfolios, and observing heated community battles over misunderstood practices in early childhood education, we have come to believe that the most important persons to include in the ten-step portfolio process are parents. Precisely because parents (and grandparents, guardians and other family members) can care so much about their children's progress, changes such as the ten-step portfolio process may be puzzling or even alarming to them. Therefore, sensitive, careful family involvement in the implementation of portfolios is critical to their success.

Particularly in kindergarten and primary programs, it can be a mistake to assume that parents or the local community will discard the traditional assessment system of report cards for portfolios without a great deal of explanation and involvement. In public school programs, school board members must be involved from the very first in any school reform efforts. By involving board members early in the process, actual approval of policy changes will be smoother. However, effective community involvement extends far beyond the school board. As the Association for Supervision and Curriculum Development puts it, "What's needed is public engagement: a much closer relationship between schools and community members than in the past, with *fuller communication* and more public input at all stages of reform" (1995, p. 3) (italics are ours).

We have suggested specific strategies for family involvement at each step in the portfolio process, beginning with development of a portfolio policy, when parents can serve on a task force or study group to discuss and draft the portfolio policy. Those parents can continue to serve as messengers for the implementation process, with each member organizing another small group of parents and community members, along with at least one knowledgeable teacher, to come together and learn about portfolio-based assessment in the context of the program's or school district's overall mission. Small groups engaged in ongoing discussion can anticipate problems with implementation, spread the good news about school

The Portfolio Book

successes and even stimulate formation of still more small groups. (By contrast, large public meetings are tempting to "agitators" who may want to dominate the program with complaints and accusations that may not even relate to assessment reform.) You can organize the small groups according to classes, neighborhoods or through informal networking. Provide refreshments for everyone who attends plus qualified caregivers for children who come along and effective materials and activities for them. You may even want to plan a round of small-group meetings before implementation of each new portfolio step.

The local news media is another vehicle for engaging parents and community members throughout the ten-step portfolio process. Use a positive, friendly theme, such as "See How We're Learning!", for a series of news advisories about children's achievements. Work samples, photographs and even systematic records can be very effective illustrations for announcements about special curriculum projects, for example. Keep the focus on what and how the children are learning—not on how you are changing assessment techniques. (Also remember to review your school's or program's policy about using children's work. Get permission when appropriate.)

The three-way portfolio conference (Step 9—pages 124–130) is also an opportunity for invaluable give-and-take with parents. Even with advance preparation, many parents will expect a traditional parent-teacher conference, with a quick run-down of the child's successes and failures and some kind of indication of how the child compares to other children in the program. It takes time to guide parents toward understanding their own children's progress in different ways. Because it is critical that you use established, clear criteria for evaluating their children's work before sharing your conclusions with parents, we urge you to proceed carefully in implementing new assessment techniques. For example, you may continue to use some multiple-choice or fill-in-the-blank tests with primary-grade children, while gradually employing various portfolio techniques to assess selected areas of learning. When you meet with parents, be sure to share the results of traditional tests as well as your findings from portfolio techniques. Careful labeling of all portfolio items is also important, so that you can easily trace their children's advances during portfolio conferences.

Involving children in the conference may also seem strange to some parents. They may not be accustomed to regarding their children as thinkers, planners and doers. During the conferences, you can subtly model appropriate ways of talking with their children about their work.

As your focus shifts to comparing the child's past and present accomplishments, and to involving the child in planning some of his own learning experiences, some parents may still want to know how their children rank. For this reason, primary programs should not suddenly abandon alpha grades. Instead, use the portfolio conference to engage parents in learning more about their own children's special strengths and needs, while continuing to record their achievements on traditional report cards. Preparing narrative reports in addition to traditional report cards can seem like a wasteful duplication of effort, but combining these accountability strategies may be the best way to prevent public opposition to assessment reform.

Even in the best of situations, there may be opposition to changes in your current assessment system. Parents or community leaders may demand, "Why do we have to change something we've done for thirty years?" or "Grades were used when I was in school. If it was good enough then, why isn't it good enough now?" To answer these questions, teachers, administrators and school board members (in primary programs) should rely on the small study groups: parents talking to parents about how portfolios help them know more about their children. Look at parents' concerns and questions as opportunities to better engage them in their children's education.

More serious opposition can come from political groups that attack assessment reform in order to undermine public education in general. Over the last few years, the politics of educating young children has become ugly. Name-calling and personal attacks on educators seeking to move schools forward have been used by many organizations, a few even claiming to act in the name of religion. These accusations have generated undue concern in many local communities, with tales of governmental intervention and federal monitoring of children's progress causing alarm and unnecessary friction between schools and families. If this type of opposition develops in your community, the following steps may be helpful:

1. Determine whether the opposition is organized.

2. Find out the sources of information the opponents are using.

3. Identify the opponents' leaders and request a meeting with them. Take a confident teacher and a committed, supportive parent along for the meeting.

4. During the meeting with opponents, explain the policy-making process and the involvement of local parents and teachers that preceded implementation of portfolios.

5. Provide authentic examples from local classrooms of portfolios in practice. A series of work samples or learning log entries can be dramatic evidence of the benefits of portfolios. (Obtain children's and parents' permission before using any such items.)

6. Seek to inform and explain, but do not compromise the portfolio policy developed by your learning community.

Final Thoughts

In the preparation and writing of this book, we talked with many teachers. Some were novices at using portfolios; others were experts. Our discussions revealed that while the ten steps we describe here are a guide to the mechanics of portfolio-based assessment, a true understanding of the need for portfolios comes to each teacher, parent and child as they become more engaged in learning through the portfolio-based assessment process; however, respecting the intellect of young

The Portfolio Book

children and trusting their ability to participate in their own education is not a step-by-step process. It is a fundamental belief system, a faith in the child and family as the center of the community of learners.

Asking young children questions as simple as, "How did you make that block bridge?" or "How is playdough different from clay?" or "What did you learn when you observed the tadpoles?" enables teachers, parents and children to collaborate in establishing learning criteria. This kind of give-and-take can lead to profound, incremental changes. One theme prevailed in our interviews with teachers and caregivers: establishing criteria for evaluating children's progress, and articulating the relationship of those criteria to conventional grading systems, is the greatest challenge of assessment reform. The teachers who have used portfolios for the longest time freely admitted that portfolio-based assessment is a process of continuous professional development. There are lessons, mistakes and surprises along the way. Techniques that work beautifully in one center or school may fail in another. Some teachers have revised and reworked portfolio techniques until they barely resemble their first attempts. Others found that some of the old ways were not all bad; some teachers have told us that they eventually realized that their dislike for alpha grades was actually a sense of their own failure in involving children in establishing the criteria for evaluating work.

We hope that our ideas about how to implement portfolios in early childhood programs challenge you to think about all aspects of your work as early childhood educators. We hope that you will think about the many ways to support young children's development, and to assess, evaluate and report their progress. As you continue to explore and learn, share your experiences with children, parents and colleagues. Analyze portfolio items and use them to explain your classroom practices. Reflection and communication are the critical activities in a community of learners, both within the walls of the preschool, family day care home or school and outside. Portfolios can foster richer, deeper, continuous reflection and communication in your community. Good luck!

References

Association for Supervision and Curriculum Development. (1995). Responding to public opinion; Reforming schools in a climate of skepticism. *Education Update* 37(5):1,3.

Evans, P. M. (1994). Getting beyond chewing gum and book covers. *Education Week* 14(7):44, 34.

Winograd, P., Jones, D., and Perkins, F. (1994). *The Politics of Portfolios, Performance Events and Other Authentic Assessments*. Lexington, KY: Institute on Education Reform, University of Kentucky. (UKERA #0007. Available from Institute on Education Reform, 101 Taylor Education Bldg., University of Kentucky, Lexington, KY, 40506-0001.)

Appendix
Glossary
Forms
Equipment List

Index

Glossary

Assessment: Any method of collecting information about the current status of an individual child, a group or sample of children, a program or a professional.

Alternative assessment: Any and all assessments that differ from the multiple-choice, timed, one-shot approaches that characterize most standardized and many classroom assessments.

Anecdotal record: A brief account of a child's action. Anecdotes describe incidents factually and objectively, including how, when and where the event occurred. Such records are typically used as evidence of unanticipated developments in individual children's progress.

Authentic assessment: This term conveys the idea that "assessments should engage students in applying knowledge and skills in the same way they are used in the "real" world outside of school. Authentic assessment also reflects good instructional practice, so that teaching to the test is desirable.

Authentic work sample: A product of a child's work that reflects real situations and problems addressed in the learning environment, rather than contrived instructional situations.

Baseline sample: Selected work collected at the beginning of the child's school experience for the purpose of assessing the current level of development in a specific area or learning domain.

Conference: A meeting between teacher and child—or teacher, child and parent(s)—to discuss specific progress in specific areas.

Dictation: The process of stating information verbally for another to record, used in early childhood settings to enable emerging writers to record their ideas.

Documentation: Preservation of information gained through classroom observation and record keeping over time.

Domain: Any area of development, such as social-emotional, cognitive or physical.

Evaluative language: Comments that reflect judgments, in this case by a caregiver, teacher, parent or other observer of young children.

Expressive language: Language that manifests or symbolizes something else. Young children demonstrate expressive language through their ability to express ideas and emotions.

Interview: An occasion when a teacher or caregiver and child discuss a project or piece of work, either completed or in process; a story or book read by the child; or any other activity, for the purpose of the adult assessing the child's development insofar as that activity can demonstrate development. The interview is a technique for probing deeply into what a child knows and can do.

Journal: A personal record of one's experiences and ideas.

Learning log: A type of record, resembling a diary, that preserves evidence of an individual child's progress in experiencing and mastering specific curriculum objectives.

Learning log conference: A regular conference between an individual child and adult in which they review recent learning activities and set new learning goals. Information from the conference is preserved in the learning log.

Narrative report: A clear written summary of a child's progress in all developmental domains during a designated period of assessment.

Naturalistic assessment: Informal observation that occurs in the natural setting of the classroom.

Pass-along portfolio: A collection of work samples, narrarive reports and other key evidence, intended to be forwarded to future teachers for the purpose of providing a continuous assessment record.

Performance assessment: A broad term that encompasses many of the characteristics of both authentic and alternative assessment.

Performance task: An assignment for a child to complete for the purpose of assessing the child's mastery of particular knowledge or skills.

Portfolio: A purposeful collection of work over time.

Portfolio-based assessment: The use of portfolios as the foundation of an array of assessment strategies. While individual assessment techniques serve different individual purposes, the portfolio supports the overall assessment and instruction of the individual child.

Portfolio conference: A meeting between a teacher and child (and perhaps a parent) to discuss the child's progress as documented through the collection of items in the child's portfolio.

Portfolio conference summary: A clear written summary of discussion, evidence and plans considered during a portfolio conference. The summary is usually a collaborative effort of the child, teacher and (perhaps) parent.

Portfolio policy: A brief set of guidelines for collecting items for preservation. Formulation of the policy begins with examination of the program's mission or goals.

Primary source: Information that is in its original form, rather than secondary, or evaluated, form. In early childhood assessment, primary sources include children's work samples, interviews with parents and observations by teachers, while secondary sources include items such as completed checklists and evaluations by other teachers.

Representational: A type of drawing which depicts real objects, persons, animals, etc. In early childhood, representational drawing follows the scribble stage, during which the child masters the use of the media.

Running record: Descriptive narrative that is more detailed than an anecdotal record. Running records are a continuous written record of everything that a child does during a designated time period.

Schematic: A type of drawing in which boundaries are evident. In young children's drawings, the schematic stage is typically evident in drawings that include sky at the top and ground at the bottom, or perhaps the wall of a bedroom or kitchen. Preschematic drawings lack these arrangements.

Secondary source: Evaluations of primary sources. In early childhood assessment, this includes comments attached to work samples, narrative reports, etc.

Standardized measurement: Measurement according to a standard, such as the expectation that a child of five years should have mastered particular skills.

Standardized testing: The use of a test to assess an individual or a group's achievement according to certain standards.

Systematic observation: Regular, deliberate and thoughtful listening, watching and recording of a child's behavior for the purpose of determining the child's progress in a particular developmental domain and area.

Systematic record: A written account of a systematic observation.

Teaching journal: A teacher's or caregiver's personal record of teaching experiences. This type of journal supports reflection and self-evaluation.

Work sample: A sample of a person's work that is preserved as evidence of the person's learning over time.

Reference

Marzano, R. J., Pickering, D., and McTighe, J. (1993). *Assessing Student Outcomes: Performance Assessemnt Using the Dimensions of Learning Model*. Alexandria, VA: Association for Supervision and Curriculum Development.

Child's Work Sample Comments

Child _____ Date _____

Piece _____

How I Did This Piece:

What I Like About It:

What I Wish I Could Change About It:

Do I Want To Try This Again?

Child's Work Sample Comments

Child _____ Date _____

Piece _____

How I Did This Piece:

What I Like About It:

What I Wish I Could Change About It:

Do I Want To Try This Again?

Child's Work Sample Comments

Child _____ Date _____

Piece _____

How I Did This Piece:

What I Like About It:

What I Wish I Could Change About It:

Do I Want To Try This Again?

Child's Work Sample Comments

Child _____ Date _____

Piece _____

How I Did This Piece:

What I Like About It:

What I Wish I Could Change About It:

Do I Want To Try This Again?

Teacher's Work Sample Comments

Child _____ Date _____
Piece _____

☐ Teacher-initiated   ☐ Child-initiated

Skill /Concept: _____

Reference: _____

☐ Beginning   ☐ Developing

☐ Mastery   ☐ Extended

Notes:

Teacher's Work Sample Comments

Child _____ Date _____
Piece _____

☐ Teacher-initiated   ☐ Child-initiated

Skill /Concept: _____

Reference: _____

☐ Beginning   ☐ Developing

☐ Mastery   ☐ Extended

Notes:

Teacher's Work Sample Comments

Child _____ Date _____
Piece _____

☐ Teacher-initiated   ☐ Child-initiated

Skill /Concept: _____

Reference: _____

☐ Beginning   ☐ Developing

☐ Mastery   ☐ Extended

Notes:

Teacher's Work Sample Comments

Child _____ Date _____
Piece _____

☐ Teacher-initiated   ☐ Child-initiated

Skill /Concept: _____

Reference: _____

☐ Beginning   ☐ Developing

☐ Mastery   ☐ Extended

Notes:

Photograph Release Form

I/we the parent(s) and/or guardians(s) of _____ grant permission

for photographs of our child to be used for informational and professional development

purposes by _____.
                              (program's name)

I/we hereby represent that I/we have the legal right to issue such consent.

Signature: _____ Date: _____

Signature: _____ Date: _____

Names (print): _____

Names (print): _____

Name _____   Teacher _____

Date _____   Grade _____

I have been learning about:

_____

_____

_____

_____

I want to learn more about:

_____

_____

_____

_____

I plan to:

_____

_____

_____

_____

Teacher's Comments: _____

_____

_____

_____

Learning Log Form

Systematic Record

Child: _____ Date: _____

Recorder: _____ Time: _____ to _____

Permission for Observation Granted by _____

Activity or Behavior:

Setting:

Details:

Reason for Observation:

Comments:

Systematic Record

Child: _____ Date: _____

Recorder: _____ Time: _____ to _____

Permission for Observation Granted by _____

Activity or Behavior:

Setting:

Details:

Reason for Observation:

Comments:

Anecdotal Record

Child _____ Date _____

Event:

Setting:

Details:

Comments:

Recorder: _____

Anecdotal Record

Child _____ Date _____

Event:

Setting:

Details:

Comments:

Recorder: _____

Anecdotal Record

Child _____ Date _____

Event:

Setting:

Details:

Comments:

Recorder: _____

Anecdotal Record

Child _____ Date _____

Event:

Setting:

Details:

Comments:

Recorder: _____

Child: _____ Date: _____

News Flash!

I observed the following incident today and thought you would want to know:

_____
Teacher

Observation is an important part of our assessment system. We learn more about how children are growing and learning by observing them often. I will share more news about your child's progress with you at our next conference, but please call me any time you have questions.

Remember that I'm always interested in news from home about your child's activities! Please encourage your child to share news of special experiences at school during class discussions or in his or her journal.

Child: _____ Date: _____

News Flash!

I observed the following incident today and thought you would want to know:

_____
Teacher

Observation is an important part of our assessment system. We learn more about how children are growing and learning by observing them often. I will share more news about your child's progress with you at our next conference, but please call me any time you have questions.

Remember that I'm always interested in news from home about your child's activities! Please encourage your child to share news of special experiences at school during class discussions or in his or her journal.

Child: _____ Date: _____

News Flash!

I observed the following incident today and thought you would want to know:

_____
Teacher

Observation is an important part of our assessment system. We learn more about how children are growing and learning by observing them often. I will share more news about your child's progress with you at our next conference, but please call me any time you have questions.

Remember that I'm always interested in news from home about your child's activities! Please encourage your child to share news of special experiences at school during class discussions or in his or her journal.

Child: _____ Date: _____

News Flash!

I observed the following incident today and thought you would want to know:

_____
Teacher

Observation is an important part of our assessment system. We learn more about how children are growing and learning by observing them often. I will share more news about your child's progress with you at our next conference, but please call me any time you have questions.

Remember that I'm always interested in news from home about your child's activities! Please encourage your child to share news of special experiences at school during class discussions or in his or her journal.

Sample Format for Parent Letter

Dear Parents:

Our children's learning portfolios are collections of important information from a variety of sources. One of our most important sources is you! I want to learn as much as possible from you about your child's interests and activities, so that I can make our learning experiences here meaningful for the children.

Please help by telling me about your children. Here are a few questions which you can answer, or you may tell me about a different area of your child's learning and growth. Please bring this information to the upcoming three-way portfolio conference. We will add your letters to your children's portfolios. I am anxious to learn from you!

Tell me about your child's favorite game.

_____

_____

_____

Tell me about a time of day or week when your child enjoys talking with you.

_____

_____

_____

Tell me about any chores that your child performs at home.

_____

_____

_____

Tell me about one or more of your child's current interests—the topics that your child talks with you about. They can be silly or serious. (Of course, we don't want you to tell us your child's secrets.)

_____

_____

_____

Thank you again for taking the time to share what you know about your child's learning and growth with me.

_____
Teacher

Equipment List

The Ten-Step Portfolio Process does not require any unusual equipment or equipment that is difficult to use. You can obtain all of these items at a discount department store or an office supply store.

1. A planner datebook or a spiral-bound notebook with plenty of room for making notes under different headings.

2. Good pens that are comfortable for you to use. Buy them by the box.

3. #2 pencils.

4. Small spiral notebooks in a size and shape that is comfortable for you to use. Buy them in quantity. If you are left-handed, use a notebook with the spirals at the top.

5. Three-prong folders for learning logs—one for each child.

6. Containers for portfolios—three for each child: a small one for the private portfolio, a large one for the learning portfolio and a smaller one for the pass-along portfolio.

7. Word processor—not essential, but very useful for composing narrative reports and other documentation.

8. Camera—not essential, but highly recommended. The features that are important in a camera for portfolio-based assessment are:

   ✓ 35 millimeter camera ("Instant" cameras often do not produce high quality photographs and are very expensive to operate. Worst of all, the photographs cannot be duplicated because there are no negatives.)

   ✓ Zoom lens with moderate wide angle and moderate telephoto, enabling you to shoot from across a room and focus on a single child or capture a group.

   ✓ Good, reliable autofocus (not too sophisticated or it may be more difficult to use).

   ✓ Good flash recycle time, which is how quickly the camera is ready to flash again.

   ✓ The option to show the date on each photograph.

   A camera like this will cost from $100 to $300. This may seem expensive, but such a camera will serve every component of your early childhood program: assessment and evaluation, curriculum planning, family involvement, even public relations. A parent in your program who is a professional photographer may be able to help you find a bargain in a used camera.

9. A supply of 35 millimeter film. For economy and convenience, you can purchase film and processing services from a mail-order company. These companies' prices are competitive and their delivery time is usually very prompt. Usually, you can pop a roll of film in the mail on Friday and have the prints back by Wednesday. You can even set up an account with one of these companies so the bills go directly to a credit card and you don't have to write a check every time you send in a roll of film. Of course, if a parent in your program has a photography lab, you can ask about discounts for your program.

10. Audiocassette recorders (as small a model as you can afford)—with reasonable care, the recorder should last for years and the only ongoing expense will be batteries.

11. A supply of audiocassettes—at least one tape for each child.

12. Plastic storage bins for audiocassettes.

Index